THE HAPPIEST
REFUGEE

• • •

For my mother and father.
And for Suzanne, my wife, my love.

THE HAPPIEST REFUGEE

The extraordinary true story of a boy's journey from
starvation at sea to becoming one of Australia's
best-loved comedians

Anh Do

● ● ●

ALLEN&UNWIN

First published in 2010

Allen & Unwin
83 Alexander Street
Crows Nest NSW 2065
Australia
Phone: (61 2) 8425 0100
Email: info@allenandunwin.com
Web: www.allenandunwin.com

Cataloguing-in-Publication details are available
from the National Library of Australia
www.trove.nla.gov.au

ISBN 978 1 74237 238 9

Set in 12/16 pt Bembo by Midland Typesetters, Australia
Printed and bound in Australia by Griffin Press

90 89 88 87 86 85

• Prologue •

I'm flying down the Hume Highway at 130 kilometres an hour. I've lost control a few times but the *brrrrrr* of those white guide things on the side of the road keep me on track. A steering wheel wet from tears is a very slippery object. I am sobbing uncontrollably.

Will he even recognise me? If he doesn't, I'm going to just turn around and walk the other way.

I haven't seen my father in nine years. Since I was thirteen in fact. I watched him walk out the door one night and haven't seen or heard from him since, except for one strange phone call late at night on my eighteenth birthday. He was drunk and I hung up. I hated him when he was drunk . . . I feared him even.

Now, here I am at the age of twenty-two rushing headlong to see him. I'm quite a lot taller than when he left. And, more importantly, stronger. I can take him now . . . easy. I'm torn between fantasies of a happy reunion with this guy and beating him up.

I'm considering the different ways I could head-butt the little Vietnamese prick. As soon as he opens the door—*Bang!* Try and get him before he has a chance to do anything. Blood would pour from his nose and he'd be sorry. I'd make him pay for everything. For pissing off. For forcing Mum to look after three kids on an illiterate Vietnamese migrant's wages of less than ten bucks an hour. But I also miss him dearly.

I remember him as funny and charming, and he taught me that I could do anything. He used to tell me, 'If you find the right woman, don't muck around and waste any time. Marry her. You'll be happy for the rest of your life. Just look at me and your mum.'

That's what he taught me. What a hypocrite.

I turn into his street and the first thing I notice is the excessive amount of graffiti in the area. It's housing commission, and the lower-end kind. Broken fences, kids running around who need a bath and front yards that haven't been mowed in a year.

I look down at the address scribbled on the back of a shop-a-docket. Number four slash fifty-two. I get out of my car and look back at my hub caps, wondering if I'm going to see them again. In front of me is a dirty looking unit that is falling apart. I check that my eyes are dry and take one enormous sniff to clear my nostrils, immediately gagging at the stench of cat piss. As I knock tentatively I can hear a baby screaming.

The grey door opens and there's a woman. She looks about twenty-five. A part of me thinks that maybe I've got the wrong place, but a part of me knows she probably has something to do with him. She looks me up and down nervously.

'Tam!' she calls out. Then he appears.

My father. Just as I remember him. Almost exactly the same. Skinny little face, slightly wonky teeth and those dark eyes that can make you know you're loved and make you shit yourself at the same time.

He grabs my neck. 'Anh! Son!' He is beaming a huge smile. 'Son!'

He starts to slap me round the head. 'Look how big you are! Look how tall you are!' He laughs hysterically. 'My god, he's huge', he squeaks to the woman.

He grabs the back of my head and pulls me inside.

A million things are going on in my mind. *Is this baby his kid? Who the hell's this woman? What a shitty place. Something stinks. Aren't I supposed to head-butt this guy?*

'You hungry?' he says.

You hungry? He always used to say that. He'd pick me up from school and the first thing he'd ask is, 'You hungry?' He'd stop the car and we'd buy a kebab on the way home. A wave of familiarity and comfort hits me like a punch in the face.

'Go fetch a beer', he says to the woman. 'And some food.'

'I'm all right', I mutter.

'You're huge!' he screams. He reaches across the plastic table and slaps me on the face. Just toyingly, but hard. He always used to slap me on the face out of affection, but always too hard.

She comes back with two beers. It's 9.30 in the morning.

Bugger it, I need a bloody beer.

So we start drinking and he's acting like nothing ever happened. He's acting like I've been away for a jolly backpacking year overseas and have just arrived home.

I put on a façade of conversation, even intermittently laughing and feigning enjoyment. Or am I feigning? I'm not sure. What I do know is that I am wrestling inside with confusion and seething with anger and hatred and violence.

I also notice that something is not a hundred per cent. My father's bravado is there, and he is smiling and laughing and as loud as ever, but something is not quite right. His speech is slightly off. Every now and then he pauses a little too long. It's not long before I learn that my father has a tumour in his head.

Just perfect. Just what I need. A baby half-brother, a stepmum who's around my age and a self-destructive dickhead of an ex-dad who might die soon. This is too much to deal with, and I figure I'll visit just this once and then let the whole thing go, like a bad dream that never happened.

I ask Dad, 'So, what's the kid's name?'

'His name is Anh. I named him after you.'

• One •

Downtown Saigon is a tangle of bikes, pedestrians and rickshaws. The year is 1976 and the Vietnam War has just ended. A crowd of people wait at the end of Phu Street, where the train tracks curve sharply around a bend.

A young girl of twenty-one, dressed traditionally in long cotton pants and a commoner's shirt, grips her bag with both hands, takes a deep breath and steels herself for the run.

The locomotive screeches into view and abruptly slows down to turn the corner. The girl and the gathered crowd start sprinting, jostling for the best positions to jump onto the slowed down train.

The girl chucks her bag into the train compartment then runs as fast as she can, trying to grab hold of the doorway. Back on the straight the train begins to speed up, she is not going to make it. The bag of snacks and fruit that she needs to sell to support her mother, five younger siblings, as well as her father and two older brothers who are locked away in communist 're-education' camps, is on that train. Her family is depending on her. She keeps sprinting and makes one last desperate attempt to grab the doorway, loses her grip and her heart plummets.

Suddenly a hairy brown arm reaches out the door and grabs her elbow. She holds her breath, leaps and the brown arm yanks her into the speeding train. She stands up and straightens her clothes, picks up her bag and thanks the owner of the arm—a smiling squat middle-aged man with a cigarette where his two front teeth should be. She then starts her day's work.

Up until 1975 when the communists took over, it was legal for traders to sell goods on the trains in Saigon. But since the end of the war the communists have made all trade that isn't documented with government papers illegal.

The girl has just finished a sale when the passengers around her start making the coughing noises that signal the guards are coming. She sits down quickly and tries to look as inconspicuous as possible.

'Tickets!'

She hears an unfamiliar voice; there must be new guards. She watches as one of them hassles an old man. The first thing you must remember when you start this kind of work is to give the guards some money or goods to soften their eyesight, so they don't see the bulge on your ankle where you've strapped packets of cigarettes or peanuts or whatever it is you're selling. And you have to do this ever so carefully, otherwise a real stickler-for-the-rules kind of guard might dob you in for bribery. Then you're really in trouble, much more than if you got caught selling stuff in the first place. It is all truly frightening. A bloody and merciless war has just finished and the murky, ugly rules of a stain-covered jungle now apply. The girl knows that people sometimes disappear for no reason.

The two new guards don't take to the old man's offerings. The girl knows she can't just get up and walk away, as that would bring attention to her. So she sits as still as she can, drawing back a little even, behind an old woman and her chicken cages.

Suddenly one of the guards, who's face is pockmarked, glances across and notices this young girl with her jet-black long hair and fair skin. He struts over to her.

'Lift up your trousers!' the guard demands.

The girl lifts up her black cotton pants to her ankles.

'Lift them up higher', he leers. 'In fact, take them off.'

Good one, she thinks to herself. *Now I'm in trouble.*

Any young twenty-one-year-old girl would be scared at that moment, but this particular girl had been enrolled in a convent until earlier that year. She was supposed to be a nun by now, but the communists had closed down all the catholic churches and convents.

What am I going to do? she wonders.

'Oi!' comes a voice from the back carriage. Not, 'Excuse me', or 'Stand back', or anything noble like that. Just a very common and working-class 'Oi', and it emanates from the fifty-five-kilogram frame of a skinny, twenty-one-year-old Vietnamese boy, with a flat nose, wonky teeth and a mop of hair that looks like he's been sleeping on one side since he was five. He's not particularly handsome, not tall or striking, and his voice isn't deep or resonant. In fact he sounds a little squeaky. But what he is, is loud. And confident. And full of 'everyone can get stuffed'. Most importantly, he is acting in defiance of the guards and in defence of her.

She is in love.

This youngster oozes bravado and pure unadulterated certainty. He seems to lack fear. And he says to these two guards in his squeaky voice, 'That's not the way to treat a young lady'.

The guard turns and looks at the skinny boy and the gang of lads behind him.

'Umm, ahhh, she was . . . I thought she might've been selling stuff, but I can't see anything, so I must be mistaken.' The guard lifts up the girl's bag of goods and places it on the seat next to her.

'I'm sorry, ma'm', and he hurries away.

The skinny young man tips his hat to this young lady and heads off through to the next carriage on his business.

The next day they both go back to the second-last carriage of the 4.30 p.m. to see if the other one is there. On their third meeting he buys her a lemonade and makes a young guy in the carriage stand up so that she can sit down. He does the same for old ladies and old men as well, people he doesn't even know.

Six months later this former nun-to-be finds herself married to this outlaw, and nine months after that they become my mum and dad.

My mother has seven brothers and sisters. She was third of the eight. When the war ended her two older brothers, high-ranking paratroopers who had fought alongside American and Australian soldiers, were put into communist 're-education' camps. The propaganda was that they would learn about the new way of life they would experience under the communist government. In truth these were more like concentration camps. Uncle Thanh jokes that it was like staying at a 'minus-five star hotel'. That brown thing on your pillow wasn't a chocolate. My uncles went in thinking they would be out in two weeks; but they were there for three years. Better than some of their mates, who never came out at all.

Uncle Thanh is Mum's eldest brother, a softly spoken man whose gentleness masks an incredible inner strength. During his re-education the communists sent Uncle Thanh into the jungle as part of a labour gang. After several months of trudging through mosquito-infested swampland and daily back-breaking work, hacking through dense vegetation, he contracted malaria. He became delirious and passed out. The guards dragged him back to the camp jail and dumped him at the infirmary tent. They had no medicine to treat malaria.

The camp's overworked doctor and his fifteen-year-old assistant placed Uncle Thanh on a stretcher and carried him, along with a couple of vats of saltwater, to a sunlit patch of jungle where the light was better. They yanked off his shirt and tied him spread out on the stretcher. The kid shoved a thick chunk of bark between my uncle's teeth so he wouldn't bite off his tongue. The doctor pulled out his rusty scalpel, dunked it in the saltwater and sliced open the prisoner's stomach. With no anaesthetic. A sickening scream whipped through the trees.

Then Uncle Thanh passed out. He didn't see the doctor carefully pull out his intestines and other organs from his stomach cavity and place them in the vat of saltwater. This treatment was supposed to sterilise the organs and purge the body of malaria. After a few minutes the doctor put them back into his stomach cavity and quickly sewed the gaping wound shut with a needle and thread, as if he were patching up a hole in his army coat.

For the next twenty-four hours Uncle Thanh hovered between life and death. He was taking up valuable space in the infirmary and the guards had to make a decision. As he looked dead enough they put him in a coffin in the makeshift morgue.

The following day a guard walked past and heard banging and shouting coming from the room full of dead bodies.

Jesus, one of them's alive, he thought.

He opened the door and there was Uncle Thanh lying on the dirt floor. To everyone's amazement he survived, but at a price. The operation left him infertile.

Uncle Huy is Mum's second eldest brother and he has a bigger build than Uncle Thanh. He is also the better looking of the two, if you ask my grandmother.

'Look how white he is', she says, '. . . and tall'. He stands at five foot six and a half.

While he was in the army, Uncle Huy's unit was told to catch a boat upstream to a different position. The night before they were due to leave, he and some army mates snuck out and went drinking. They got completely plastered and were late waking up the next day. As they raced down to the port they saw their boat leaving.

'We're going to get into so much trouble for this. Why didn't you wake us up you idiot!' Uncle Huy yelled, smacking his mate next to him across the back of the head.

The four soldiers watched the boat grow smaller as it moved slowly out of the harbour. As Uncle Huy reached down to pull out a cigarette he heard an enormous BANG! There was a gigantic explosion on the far side of the waterway that looked like a fireball hovering above the water. It was their boat. The friends stared, stunned and silent at the fate they had just escaped. Everyone on board was dead.

That moment affected my uncle for many years, planting the seed for his life's calling: shortly after arriving in Australia, he entered a seminary in Sydney, took his vows and became a Jesuit priest.

My father grew up in extreme poverty. His mother gave birth to twelve children but four had died in childbirth or early infancy. Even with eight mouths to feed Grandma found it in her heart to adopt two more boys. So Dad grew up as one of ten—nine boys and one girl, who was the last child, a whimsical gift to Grandma from nature.

Many large Vietnamese families have so many kids that they give them a nickname which is simply the order they were born. My dad was the fourth born. His name is Tam, but his brothers simply call him 'Four'. It was a system that evolved in poor villages where large families were common, and it just made things easier. When Grandma needed to get everyone in for dinner she would just stick her head out of the hut and shout: 'Two, Three, Four, Six, Eight . . . time to eat!'

My grandfather was in the army, so Grandma was left to look after ten kids on her own in the little hut, and they eked out an existence on one soldier's meagre wages. The family were so poor that all nine boys would sleep on the floor in a row. At night Grandma would move along and simply count the feet to make sure there were eighteen. At dinnertime each child would sit down on the dirt floor in a circle, pick up their little bowl of rice and in the middle of the circle there would be a tiny plate of sweet potato, seasoned heavily with salt so the flavour would last as long as possible with the rice. Any type of meat was a rare and special event.

One of my dad's earliest memories as a kid was receiving big pats on the back for catching three little fish from a nearby stream. Dad's father cooked them up in a broth of rice and sweet potatoes and the flavour of the fish permeated right through the vegetables. It was one of the best meals of his childhood.

One afternoon during the war my father was walking home with his brother, Six, one of the adopted boys, and they found themselves in the middle of Vietcong gunfire. He and his brother had to run away, literally skipping through the gunshots hitting the ground. Once they were safe, they realised that everyone else had fled the village and they were alone. They noticed a huge plum tree nearby. Dad had had his eye on this tree for some time and he really hated the idea that these Vietcong soldiers would get to enjoy its fruit. He and Uncle Six climbed the tree and picked as many plums as they could, wrapped them up in their shirts and took them home. That afternoon all ten siblings feasted on as many plums as they could eat—my uncles still talk fondly about the famous 'plum banquet'.

Uncle Thanh and Uncle Huy had been in the re-education camp for three years, and during that time saw many prisoners die around them. Some died of sickness, some of starvation, some were executed. My uncles had misrepresented their true rank in the army to their captors; playing down their role because they were fearful of the repercussions. They spent their time in the camps terrified of what might happen if the truth became known. My mum was understandably anxious about her brothers and my father could see that his young wife was worried. As usual Dad decided to take matters into his own hands.

The strange thing about civil wars is that often good friends and, sometimes, even family end up on opposite sides. Dad had a friend called Vu, whose uncle had become a high-ranking communist official. Dad had known Vu just about all his life and he asked a huge favour of his friend: 'Vu, when your uncle goes north next week, I need you to sneak in and borrow a uniform and some paperwork for me.'

One sunny afternoon my father walked into the remote re-education camp dressed as a high-ranking communist officer. He marched right through the front door of the commanding officer's room.

'These two men need to come with me', he demanded. The commanding officer was bewildered. He was afraid to disobey such a high-ranking official so he did not resist. My father then walked my uncles out of the camp, right through the front gate.

My mother's family were stunned, and of course delighted to have their sons home again. Their son-in-law may have been skinny with wonky teeth, but his bravery, in the face of extreme danger, was breathtaking.

• Two •

My extended family pooled all their money, called in favours with friends and relatives and sold everything they had—every possession— just to buy a boat. Getting your hands on a boat was an extremely risky business. They were only available on the black market and anyone caught trying to buy one could be jailed or killed. After a couple of false starts they finally managed to acquire a small vessel.

It was old and creaky and stank of fish. Sleeping quarters were basic—a few wooden benches in a cabin just under the water-line. If nature called, you would have to deal with it in a bucket or over the edge. The deck had long wooden seats on one side, where the youngsters and older family members could rest. If you wanted protection from the elements, you had to go below. Everyone would be exposed to the sun and wind.

The boat was nine metres long by two and a half metres wide and there would be forty people crowded on board—immediate family, uncles (including the two who had been in the camps for three years), aunts and friends, including toddlers, babies and teen-agers whose parents were too old or sick to make the journey. No belongings would be taken except the clothes on their backs, though everyone had been stockpiling food and water for months. There wasn't a lot but enough to last the week they expected to be at sea. Any leftover funds were swapped for small amounts of gold, the 'international currency', in the hope that wherever we ended up it could be traded for local money.

My dad and uncles had spent hours huddled together at night planning the escape. The goal was to reach Malaysia and the journey was going to be complicated and potentially life threatening.

There was a canal system around the village where our family lived and a smaller boat would have to be inconspicuously navigated through the waterways to reach the main boat. My father, then twenty-five years old, was designated captain of the boat because he was the only one who knew how to navigate the small waterways to get out to sea.

Dad's skills had been finely honed. He had previously sold coal at the markets at 4 a.m. every morning and had to navigate his way through the canals to get there. Each day as he went off to work the sky was pitch-black and there was always a prevailing crosswind, which made it easy to crash the boat along the way. He would watch small patches of reflections from moonlight on the leaves of trees lining the bank. He could tell by the play of light whether to guide the canoe forward or turn it sideways.

The day of our departure arrived and Dad woke in the early hours. Many of our family members who were going on the boat had stayed at Grandma's house the night before departure, because it was near the canals. The house was still dark but Dad could hear murmuring in the women's room. He tiptoed to the door and could just make out the dim outline of his mother kneeling, hands clasping her rosary beads. Several months before, she had lost two of her sons in their quest to leave Vietnam. She was now praying for her children who were departing that day. Dad felt grief and guilt at having to leave her behind. He also felt a surge of fear as he remembered the fate of the journey that had taken the lives of brothers Five and Seven.

Dad came into our room and in the darkness kissed his wife and two sleeping sons.

'*Bo Thoung Con Qua.*' I love you, my sons.

He then tiptoed through the house and stepped out into the cold night air, bracing himself for his last day in Vietnam.

Our group of forty did not head out together that day. Starting early, under cover of darkness, we set off in groups of three or four in small motorised canoes that were usually used for carrying food to the morning markets. This process took many hours because the main boat, 'the Motherfish', was so far away, the canoes had to follow different convoluted routes through the canals so that they didn't attract attention. The communists were on the alert for potential boat people and everyone knew there was a chance you could get stopped and caught by the army. If anyone stopped them, they would say they were going out to their fishing boat in the bay.

Mum and my baby brother, Khoa, left on one of the first canoes. Dad's brother, Uncle Eight, piloted the boat while Mum and Khoa hid inside the tiny little steerage hatch. Uncle Eight hoisted several big heavy bags of corn into the boat and used them to cover the opening of the hatch so Mum and Khoa couldn't be seen. Mum stuffed chunks of sticky rice into Khoa's mouth so that he wouldn't wail at the wrong moment. This was a foolproof plan because at fifteen months of age my brother had already earned the nickname 'Fatty'. He was a very good eater.

I was two and a half years old and sent on a separate boat with Mum's brother Uncle Thanh and his wife, Aunty Huong. Dad had decided that it was too risky for Mum to take both children, in case we were too noisy. Uncle Thanh drove the boat and I hid inside the hatch with my aunty. Just as we were approaching an army patrol boat in the canal I decided that I was sick of having rice stuffed in my mouth and started crying for my mum.

'Shhhh!' Uncle Thanh hissed. 'Get him to be quiet!'

'I can't! What can I do?' panicked Aunty Huong as she jiggled me up and down and tried to cover my mouth, half-suffocating me. The more she tried, the louder I screamed.

'Here, give him this', said Uncle Thanh as he shoved his arm through the corn bags and handed my Aunty his gold wedding ring. She gave it to me, and I straight away put it into my little mouth, which freaked her out and made her forcibly pry open my jaw to retrieve the ring before I choked to death. This made me wail even louder and the patrol boat got closer still. Thankfully, just as it approached us, Uncle Thanh realised it was just a fishing boat. The group of fishermen stared at this canoe with a strange lone man who they had heard wailing like a baby, then telling himself to shush up in a woman's voice. My uncle told me later that, by the look on their faces, they knew what we were doing but just turned a blind eye.

Earlier in the day, before the rest of the boats started their trips out to the Motherfish, Dad had made his way quietly down to a little canoe at the water's edge. Dad's knowledge of the canals and his seamanship made him vital to the success of our journey—he couldn't risk being caught. He also had with him all the equipment we would need for the escape, like maps and compasses. If he were spotted the whole thing would have to be aborted.

Waiting for Dad at the boat were two teenage boys, Kiet and Toan. Dad's plan was to paddle the motor-less canoe, with the help of the two boys, fifty kilometres through the waterways and then out to the open sea. Dad and the two boys jumped into the canoe and commenced their marathon paddle.

They each took turns on the oars. As the sun rose, the heat of the day seeped into their skin and soon their shirts were drenched in sweat. When the sun was high in the sky, Dad judged that it was almost midday. Suddenly, the roar of a communist guard boat approached them from behind.

Dad quickly bent down to grab some fishing nets so he could look like he was busy mending them and whispered, 'Just remember what I told you. Keep your mouths shut and let me talk'.

The patrol boat cut its engine and idled next to the canoe. A soldier squinted down at them.

'What are you doing out here?'

'Fishing.'

A tense silence followed as the squinty-eyed face bent down to stare at Dad under his straw fishing hat. Dad held his gaze without flinching. Another voice murmured behind the soldier.

'Maybe they're going out to a boat?'

The soldier looked out at the open sea, considering.

'Ha! They'd have an engine. Only an idiot would try to paddle that far.'

And with that the communist boat roared back to life and continued on its way.

When Dad's canoe finally made it out to the Motherfish, several pairs of hands reached out and hoisted him and the two boys onto the boat. People silently cheered as their scared and nervous faces looked at their fatigued and exhausted leader. Dad reassured them with his trademarked wonky teeth smile.

The next morning was going to be the most nerve-wracking because we needed to cross the invisible border between Vietnam and international waters. Armed communists patrol boats made routine surveillance missions along this stretch. We had two engines on the Motherfish, the main one and a smaller back-up engine. Dad got both of them going to get us across this patch of sea as fast as possible.

Just when it seemed we were finally beyond the border patrol area, Uncle Eight screamed out: 'Patrol Boat!'

Behind us a patrol boat was heading in our direction at full speed. Dad cranked up both the motors to maximum thrust and we bounced violently across the waves.

Bang! Bang!

The patrol boat began shooting at us, and the women on our boat screamed.

Bang! Bang! Bang!

The patrol boat was gaining on us and Dad knew that being caught meant jail for nearly everyone on board, and possibly executions for my paratrooper uncles and himself. All of a sudden there was a loud '*Snap!*' The back-up engine stopped.

'Jesus!'

Dad steered the boat onwards with just one engine. The soldiers would surely catch us.

Suddenly Uncle Eight called out, 'They've turned back!'

Everyone went to look and he was right. The patrol boat decided not to pursue us any further outside their zone of surveillance. They now headed away from us.

'Thank you God.'

Some people started clapping and cheering. Dad shushed them all and began guiding the boat out of the bay and into the open sea. He knew there was a long, long way to go.

There was nothing but flat, blue water in every direction. The heat of the tropical afternoon sun clung to our skin and shoulders, and people tried to shield their eyes from the glare as the boat skidded along the frothy waves. The engine was spewing out thick petrol fumes and these, combined with the up-and-down motion, meant that our first few hours on-board were punctuated by bodies retching over the side of the vessel.

The boat was so small that we were jammed into every crevice, corner and spare patch of deck. It was almost impossible to get downstairs into the hold, which was heaving with sweating bodies and the suffocating stench of old fish. Forty people had transformed

this tiny fishing boat into a living, seething mass of human desperation floating in the Eastern Sea.

Forty people on a nine by two and a half metre fishing boat,
weighing the boat down so much that there was only half a metre of
mossy wood between the rails of the boat and the waterline. Every
time a big wave hit, we'd all scramble to bail out the water.

My mother, with a hot, crying child under each arm, stepped
over and around bodies and made slow progress down into the hold,
trying her best to calm two scared and delirious children. The boat's
provisions consisted mainly of rice and vegetables.

Dad and my uncles had decided we should hold off eating
until evening, not just to preserve food but to also instil a sense of
authority and discipline. By nightfall everyone was starving and
found reasons to ask for more than their tiny share, but Dad had
to be firm to make the rations last. After eating, people slumped in
whatever space they could find and tried to sleep. I cried for a while
then fell asleep next to Mum. Despite all Mum's attempts to soothe
him, Khoa screamed throughout the night.

The second day was much the same, a hot burning sun and a
horizon that stretched on forever. Later in the day, though, the
hard blue sky clouded over and gave us welcome respite from the
heat. Mum brought Khoa and me up onto the deck for some fresh
air—by now the stench of petrol fumes and old fish had combined
with vomit and human excrement to fill the hold with an unbear-
able smell.

As the afternoon wore on, the soft white cushions scudding
across the sky turned into angry grey storm clouds and the wind
whipped waves into heaving swells—our little fishing boat pitched
from side to side. With every wave that hit, water washed over us
and every able body scrambled to bail it out. Soon the sky darkened

further, turning a sinister, tumultuous black as the wind shrieked and skidded across the deck like a panicking ghost.

Mum grabbed us and shoved Khoa and me through the hatch door into the darkness of the hold and my aunty's waiting arms. Mum climbed in and looked back, taking one last anxious look at the men of her family, who were rushing and yelling, their screams torn from their throats by the howling wind. She heard Dad's strained voice—'Go Hien, *now!*'—which had an unexpected tone that she recognised as fear. She looked up to see an enormous wall of grey-green water that appeared to have swallowed the sky. It was as though the bottom of the ocean was about to crash down on top of us. She screamed and fell down the steps into the hold, the hatch door banging shut behind her.

A deafening darkness. Mum felt like a blind woman groping wildly amidst flailing arms and knees and hair, all the sounds intensified by her loss of sight. She could hear her babies screeching with terror; others were moaning, praying, shouting; wood was cracking under the full force of the sea smashing against our little wooden boat. As the boat pitched, the bodies in the hold rolled and fell from side to side. My mother managed to get hold of Khoa and me and we clung to her neck as we were shoved and pushed by the mass of limbs.

The boat righted. Mum crouched down and wrapped her arms around a wooden pole with Khoa and I still hanging on for our lives. She heard my aunty's voice faintly behind her:

Hail Mary, full of grace,
The Lord is with thee.
Blessed are thee amongst women . . .

We hung on and waited . . . and waited some more. Mum managed to keep hold of her post and her children. The boat kept pitching, the wind kept howling and people kept praying. Slowly the storm began to subside. I whimpered against my mother's chest.

My brother's crying became more audible. Mum rocked us gently on her lap.

'Shhh, shhh. It's okay now. Everything is okay.' And she sang a Vietnamese mother's lullaby to us.

> *I have Dad, I have Mum*
> *Mum loves me*
> *like a stream on a mountain top.*
> *From the moment I was born*
> *Mum nursed me like an egg*
> *Held me like a flower*
> *Cradled me in her arms...*

While she sang, she prayed that her children still have a mum and a dad.

Once the storm passed, it was strangely quiet. Waves lapped at the boat but it was as though there was no human cargo in the hold. We were scared to move, afraid of what we might find up on deck. Finally from above, the hatch door opened and light poured in to startle us from our stupor.

Mum tucked her children under her arms and shoved her way through the bodies up to the deck, her heart pounding loudly in her chest. She shielded her eyes from the glare and scanned the boat.

Uncle Thanh.

Uncle Huy.

Uncle Eight.

There they were, accounted for—two strapped to a bench, one strapped to the side of the pilothouse with rope. Not moving much, but alive.

But where is he?

Mum scanned the boat again. The glass windows of the tiny pilot-house were blown out. It was the only place left to look. Frantically,

Mum made her way across the splintered wood, broken benches and debris. She found him, bleeding from cuts to his face and arms, but okay and still standing at the helm, steering the boat back on course.

'Tam!'

'Are you okay? The boys okay?' he asked.

'Yes, yes. We're fine. Everyone's okay', Mum sobbed. 'Thank God we're all still alive.'

Much of our cooked rice was ruined by seawater, and a good portion of our fresh water supply was lost overboard in the storm. But at least we were alive. Once the weather cleared, the sun returned in full force and again we faced the choice of being cooked on the deck or crouched below in the dark, stinking hold.

There was no escaping the heat or the people. There was no space to stretch out your legs and arms. Everywhere were sweating, salty bodies with brown, dirty faces peeling from sunburn and slowly darkening.

Dad would cling onto the tiller in the tiny pilothouse and close his eyes for a few seconds, trying to steal a tiny bit of space for his own thoughts, away from the mass of people bearing down on him, asking him questions, depending on him to keep them alive. He closed his eyes and saw his mother's face, her dark eyes weary and heavy with the sadness of lost children. He saw himself in the canoe with Kiet and Toan, paddling down the canal. He remembered looking back at the shore and seeing his dog, Ki, running along beside them.

That's funny, he thought.

When he rowed the canoe to the markets to sell coal Ki had never followed him. But the dog knew. He knew something was different this time. He was a smart dog. In the mornings Dad or his brothers used to throw grain to their chickens and the neighbour's hens would come running over to eat the grain. Ki knew which chickens belonged to his own family and he would put his paw on the neighbour's chickens to stop them eating the grain. He never hurt the other chickens, just restrained them long enough, then let them go.

Yes, Ki was a smart dog, Dad smiled to himself. He wondered what would happen to his mother and his sister back at home. *Would they be okay?* Then he thought about his own family on the boat. He was responsible for the lives of his wife and two young sons, as well as his brothers, in-laws, cousins and all the others on the boat, everyone relying on this twenty-five year old to deliver them to safety.

In the middle of the second night, my father was woken by a scream. 'The kid's gone in!' Dad clambered out of the hold onto the deck. An old lady was overwrought. 'He just jumped in!'

Loc was a seventeen-year-old boy whose mother, a friend of our family, asked Dad to take him with us when we were preparing to leave Vietnam. She hoped Loc would create a better life for himself, and one day sponsor her so she could leave Vietnam too. After a few days on the boat, Loc became so feverish with all the heat, the dehydration and the vomiting that he started hallucinating and mumbling incoherent thoughts.

'Where is he?' Dad screamed.

It was pitch-black and now everyone was woken by the commotion. My uncle was manning the engine and he circled back as thirty-something pairs of eyes searched the waves for the boy, but found nothing. We searched the black water for over an hour. Loc was gone.

Another day passed. Mum carried her two exhausted children up onto the deck. It was swelteringly hot, but she needed a break from the thick stench of the hold—at least the air was fresh up top. Everyone was still and silent, the heat of the sun pushing down on us, making already hungry and thirsty human beings thirstier still, rendering us incapable of speech.

Suddenly, a distant shout broke Mum's thoughts. She shook her head and returned to the present. Yes, a man on board was shouting and waving his arms. He had seen a boat! And there it was, a small brown speck marring the smooth blue surface of the ocean. Mum's heart flooded with relief and she felt hot tears on her cheeks. *At last we will be rescued.*

Much of our food had deteriorated and our water supply was down to almost nothing, but we had survived.

Thank you God! Mum prayed silently.

We all started jumping up and down waving for this boat to come to us—thirty-nine pairs of eyes, brightened by hope, watched the brown speck's progress toward us. As it got bigger we could see it was an old fishing boat, a little larger than ours. It pulled up alongside our vessel.

Fishermen. Thank goodness. We couldn't tell where they were from, but from the insignia on their boat, maybe Thailand. We didn't care. They were going to save us. Before any of our group could figure out what was going on, the fishermen quickly jumped onto our boat.

'Sit down all of you and SHUT UP!' their leader barked.

We were quickly surrounded by seven men with knives and guns. They were pirates. They descended on us angrily, striking random faces to assert their intent, yanking off bracelets and rings from trembling hands.

They ordered all of us to take our clothes off, and we did.

Mum was standing next to Uncle Eight who looked over and saw the gold cross Grandma had given to Mum before the journey dangling around her neck. He ripped it off her and stuck it in his mouth, flicking the fake-gold chain into the ocean.

His plan was to hide the cross under his tongue but, as the pirates made their way towards him, he could see them ordering people to open their mouths, so he swallowed it.

Once they had everything of value they could see, the pirates readied to leave, except for one angry moustached pirate, who called out obscenities from the back. An old lady, Bao, had a beautiful jade bracelet that was tight around her wrist. In Vietnam it is tradition for young girls to receive one of these bracelets on their eighteenth birthday—they would put it on and never take it off. Naturally, as the girl got older, the bracelet would get tighter until it was impossible to slip beyond the hand. The pirate was tugging so hard Bao's knuckles were white, but the bracelet would not budge. He grabbed her arm and stretched it over the side of the boat. Another pirate raised his machete high up into the air . . .

My Aunty Huong stepped in and greased the old lady's wrist with a handful of day-old vomit, a makeshift lubricant. The bracelet slipped off reluctantly and Aunty handed it to the pirate in a begging stoop. They took the bracelet; they took everything, even our engine. Then they were gone, just like that.

All was still. The silence was broken only by waves lapping at our boat and an old lady's weeping.

In the back corner of the hold, covered in old rags, was one thing the pirates had missed—the second engine that had broken down during the chase. Miraculously, they'd overlooked it. Dad pulled it out and looked at the broken down motor, trying to figure out a way to mend the snapped rubber ring. He'd fixed old engines before, but without tools and equipment it all seemed hopeless.

Just then Uncle Eight wandered over to see how it was all going. Dad looked down and noticed the old pair of sandals his brother was wearing. *That's it!*

Using a knife, Dad cut a hole into the rubber sole of one of the sandals and made a round hoop, roughly the same size as the snapped rubber ring. He tested its elasticity and with a bit of shaping and re-shaping, stretched it over the engine's motor and made it fit.

Everyone watched as Dad pulled the starter cord. The engine roared to life and we all cheered. This time Dad didn't tell any of us to be quiet . . . he cheered loudest of all.

Uncle Eight was staring at the blue horizon, thinking about his mother whom he'd left behind, thinking about food, and thinking about how he was going to retrieve the cross he'd just swallowed. All of a sudden he yelled out, 'Boat!'

We all squeezed onto the deck again and looked out across the blue. This time the thirty-nine bodies dressed in dirty clothes were stiff with fear. We had no weapons and nowhere to hide. We were an exposed pimple on the vast face of the ocean. But there was still a chance, still a small amount of hope that the boat approaching us was benevolent. We might be rescued. We waited.

As the boat got closer we realised they were also pirates, but Dad could do nothing. The vessel rammed into ours and within minutes a gang of nine men were on our boat waving guns in the air and screaming.

It was too much. We stood there silent and numb, like sheep awaiting slaughter. We were forced to strip off our clothes again, and the pirates stalked up and down the rows of naked bodies, inspecting opened, trembling mouths, occasionally pulling out a gold capping. My father stated what appeared to be obvious, 'We have nothing left'.

A pirate with black front teeth leered at Aunty Huong. He muttered something and then without warning, grabbed her arm and dragged her onto the other boat.

'Huong!' Uncle Thanh screamed and lunged for his wife. A rifle butt cracked him across the back of the head. With the tip of a gun sticking into her lower back, my Aunty was pushed into the pilot-house on the pirate vessel. Black teeth was breathing heavily on her naked flesh and words tumbled from her mouth:

Hail Mary, full of grace,
The Lord is with thee.
Blessed are thee amongst women,
And blessed is the fruit of thy womb, Jesus.

Holy Mary, mother of God,
Pray for us sinners, now
And at the hour of our death . . .

Back on our boat one of the pirates grabbed hold of the smallest child. He lifted up the baby and ripped open the child's nappy. A tiny slice of gold fell out. The pirate picked up the metal and wantonly dangled the baby over the side of the boat, threatening to throw the infant in. My father screamed at the top of his lungs, 'We must save the child! We will fight to the death to SAVE THE CHILD!'

Suddenly guns were lifted and machetes raised. The robbery now turned into a full-blown standoff: nine men with weapons against thirty-seven starving refugees, a baby dangling over the ocean, and a naked woman awaiting hell.

The most dangerous animal is the one cornered and fearful. My uncles, ex-army paratroopers, suddenly felt a surge of adrenalin and stood up in unison. They were tired and hungry and weak, but they had one last fight left in them. Then the teenage boys started calling out to each other, psyching each other up, their fear now turned into desperate rage. Everyone was ready to fight till the end. If the child was thrown into the ocean, there would be no survivors.

The head pirate sized up the situation and barked frantically at the man dangling the baby. The child was thrown to the feet of his mother. His life was spared.

That baby was my brother Khoa. My crying mother gathered him up and held him tight, like a son who had returned from the dead.

One by one the pirates went back to their vessel, taking with them every little thing they could find, even our broken second engine. The pirate with black teeth angrily yanked my aunty out of the pilothouse and shoved her back onto our boat. She fell on the deck and was protectively covered by the arms and bodies of our family, grateful that nothing further had happened to her. The pirate's noisy diesel motor started up and fumes filled the air.

As their boat veered away, one of the pirates did something strange. He was a young kid according to my uncles, no more than eighteen years old, and had been less aggressive throughout the whole encounter. Suddenly and for no apparent reason he threw us a gallon of water.

That water saved our lives.

You can't drink jewellery or eat gold teeth caps, but that water meant everything because it bought us an extra day. That second pirate attack saved our lives.

Now we drifted according to the breeze, our boat a small blimp in a vast blue universe of ocean. We had been at sea for four days and that gallon of water did not last long. We lay quietly, waiting for death or a miracle.

On the fifth day Mum squinted at a distant shape. Another boat, but it looked different to the others. The boat grew bigger and bigger and bigger still. We saw a flag waving on its mast. It was a huge boat. A ship, actually. Our boatload of beaten refugees stirred and stared—waiting, hoping, but terrified to hope too much. The ship came closer and suddenly a voice blared through a loudspeaker. It was incomprehensible, shocking in its loudness. These were no Thai pirates. We looked up at a dozen fair, foreign faces. They were Germans.

The fair faces smiled down at us, giving us benevolent looks that said, 'You will be okay now'. My mother sank to her knees, clutching Khoa and me to her chest, and said, 'Thank you God.' Parched mouths murmured with excitement, tears rolled down dirty cheeks, bodies hugged and breathed great sighs of relief. It had finally come to an end.

Dad looked up at the Germans and spotted an older man with a long aquiline nose, peaked hat and many stripes on his jacket sleeve. He was obviously the captain. A torrent of foreign words poured from his mouth. We continued to gaze up at our saviours with blank, but smiling faces.

The captain dropped down behind the ship's railing for a moment and then reappeared with something in his hands. Dad couldn't quite make it out. The captain threw the object onto our boat.

Whack! A heavy axe landed on the deck. Everyone jumped, startled by the appearance of a weapon. A flicker of concern crossed Dad's face as he looked up at the captain again. The captain pointed at the axe and gesticulated with his arms. More strange words came tumbling out.

What's he saying?

Now the other sailors joined their captain in this crazy, cross-cultural game of charades. Some were pointing at our boat and some were making whacking actions with their arms, as though chopping something with an axe.

'What are they doing? Do you think they're going to attack us?' Uncle Eight asked, confused.

He was making his way across to Mum, psyching himself up to swallow that gold cross he'd only just managed to return to her that morning.

And then a flash of enlightenment.

'Maybe they can only rescue us if our boat is sinking!' shouted Dad. So he picked up the axe, swung it above his head, and struck our little wooden boat.

Thwack!

It was as though we'd finally got the secret password. Open sesame! A rope ladder appeared over the side of the ship and the sailors began pulling us on board, one by one, carefully nursing the women and children with a tenderness that will always stick in my mother's mind.

Dad, with barely enough energy left to lift the axe let alone use it properly, finally broke through the wooden hull and water began gushing in. He was the last to be taken on board and by the time he stepped off the rope ladder his dry sunburnt face had cracked open into a whopping great big smile as he tasted his own salty tears of relief. He'd delivered thirty-nine lives to safety.

• Three •

The German ship took us to a refugee camp in Pulau Bidong, an island in the Malaysian archipelago. As soon as we landed we were surrounded by other refugees. We made friends, traded stories and shared experiences, and realised that our boat had indeed been incredibly lucky. Many others had been through far greater suffering.

The second day on the island, American helicopters flew overhead and dropped bags of food. The drop contained a number of items, including lots of tins of corned beef—a practical and long-lasting food. For the first few weeks, our family indulged on this canned meat and, to this day, it is my mum's favourite food. Every second Christmas she still rolls it out and I curse those choppers for not dropping something tastier. I mean, after bombing the hell out of Vietnam, the least they could've done was thrown us some lobster.

One day a local Malaysian man came to the camp and offered to buy gold off the refugees. Mum sold her small gold cross for US$30. She got a good price after telling him that it had 'been through a very difficult passage'. Our family feasted on that sale—Khoa and I got to eat apples and drink Coca-Cola for a week.

We spent nearly three months at the Pulau Bidong refugee camp and decided we'd go to whichever country would take us. Australia eventually offered us sanctuary. Mum and Dad were overjoyed. Dad walked around the island asking people if they had any spare warm clothes. He collected a big bundle of jumpers and blankets because he'd heard about Australia—'Beautiful country, friendly people, but really cold. It's right near Switzerland.'

That's my dad, great at rescues, crap at geography. We touched down in Sydney, Australia in thirty-degree Celsius heat and my family were thinking, *Geez, Austria's really hot, man!*

August 1980. 'What a great country!' my parents said to each other. One of the first things that happened was two smiley nuns from St Vincent de Paul came and gave our family a huge garbage bag stuffed full of clothes. No charge. For free!

There were several pairs of pants for Mum, including two really nice pairs of jeans. She was in heaven. Mum had only ever seen jeans in posters for cowboy movies, and all her life had only owned two pairs of pants at any one time. Now these wrinkly old white angels came and gave her the wardrobe of a western movie star.

'Tam! Imagine a country could be so well off they could throw this stuff away', she said.

This big, black magic bag had other things too: belts and skirts and scarves. And also kids' clothes.

'Oh, how beautiful. Little tiny jeans. Tam! These people are geniuses . . . look at these for Anh!' Then Mum and Dad turned me into a little Clint Eastwood.

Somewhere in the translation, someone had mistakenly written down that we were a family with a boy and a girl. My mother, ever polite and practical, took these kind gifts with a grateful smile and, for the next few months, accepted compliments from strangers about what a 'pretty little daughter' she had. If you ever meet my brother Khoa, make sure you mention the lovely photo you saw of him in Anh's book wearing a lacy dress with gorgeous red ribbons.

And it wasn't just Khoa who experienced little mix ups with the clothes. Uncle Huy—who had a bit of a large bottom—found that a certain pair of jeans was more comfortable than the others. He walked around in them with a check-me-out, how-good-do-I-look grin on his face when my mum spotted something not quite right.

'Which side is the zip on?' she asked.

'What are you talking about?'

'Look at the zip, those are women's pants.'

'No they're not', Uncle Huy huffed, turning red. But Mum was on a roll.

'Look, the zip is on the left side. Hahhahha. Everyone look, Huy is wearing girlie pants.' She offered him a frilly hot-pink number: 'You want a nice blouse to go with that?'

'You don't even know . . . in Australia the zip can be like, on either side.' He scurried off, trying to get the pants off so quickly he caught himself in the backward zip.

A couple of months later, our family discovered that the nuns from St Vincent de Paul actually had a shop where you could go and *pick your own clothes,* buying them at a fraction of the cost. We all walked into that shop and it was like second-hand heaven. We wandered around open-mouthed saying, 'Oooh' and 'Ahh', like we were five-year-old kids. That distinctive, beautiful smell of mothballs and old clothes that have just been washed wafted into our nostrils and we were drunk with anticipation.

Uncle Dung, one of Mum's younger brothers, and the most smiley of all the uncles, stumbled onto the clearance table and shouted out to the whole shop that he had struck gold. He was literally shaking with excitement and disbelief that such a thing could even exist.

'Everyone come quickly!' he yelled. 'This table . . . *even cheaper*!!!'

He got pats on the back from his siblings: 'What a find!' In this wonderful, incredible shop where everything is already a bargain,

Uncle Dung has found the table that is bargained again. It's like cheap, minus rock bottom, divided by the square root of next to nothing.

Uncle Dung's hands were shaking as he quickly sifted through the mountain of clothes and suddenly felt an unfamiliar softness. He pulled out a fur jacket. A beautiful luxurious thick down, made of some kind of animal that must have been rare and exotic.

'Hien! Come over and try it on!'

Mum darted over and tried to squeeze into it. It didn't fit.

'I'll buy it for my girlfriend', Uncle Dung said.

'What are you talking about? You don't have a girlfriend', Uncle Thanh responded.

'If I have this I'll be able to *get one!*' He looked down at the reflection of light bouncing off the fur. 'One day, I'm going to meet a girl and give her this.'

'Put it back you idiot.'

'No!'

'What if she's fat?' Mum asked. But Uncle Dung had made up his mind.

'Nah. I'm going to buy it. It's only fifty cents.'

A couple of glorious hours of shopping later we left, and took with us an enormous loot. We felt so happy, even a little bit guilty, that we'd bought all these beautiful clothes for next to nothing. Uncle Dung was especially thrilled as one day he would meet a beautiful woman and he'd be ready for her, with his generous fifty-cent gift.

Uncle Huy was happy too. He found some men's jeans that accommodated his generous backside, which was something he was enormously proud of. He felt it made him the best looking of all the brothers.

'At least I have an arse', he'd say. 'Look at your other uncles . . . they got no arse. Look at Uncle Dung—he's got nothing. Just looks like a lower back with a hole in it.'

'What a great country!'

Almost every day we discovered something else that made Mum and Dad shake their heads at how lucky we'd been. If you got sick, you could go to the doctor for free. If you couldn't get a job straight away, the government gave you some money to help you get by.

'You listen to us, kids. As you grow up, you make sure you do as much as you can to give back to this country that gave us a second chance.'

It hadn't taken my father long to find a job in a factory, and then we were able to move out of the East Hills Migrant Hostel where we had been staying since we arrived in Sydney. Dad rented a two-bedroom flat in Marrickville. (Two bedrooms! Hah! What a great country!)

We lived above an old lady who watered the flowers in the block's common grounds, and after Dad helped her carry a bag of potting mix one day, she became our friend. Miss Buk is what we called her (I suspect her name might have been Burke, lucky for her it wasn't Furke), and she was instrumental in helping us find our feet in this exciting new world. Mum would knock on her door with a delicious plate of spring rolls, and offer them to Miss Buk along with a handful of forms which we needed help to fill in—Anh's primary school application, Dad's work forms and Mum's hospital documents when she was pregnant again.

After my little sister was born Miss Buk gave Mum a tiny white dress made of lace for the christening. She had spent several months making it and it was the most beautiful thing my Mum had ever seen. Mum and Dad turned to each other again: 'What a great country!'

It was 1982 when I started school at St Bridget's Primary, a local Catholic school with an abundant mix of nationalities: Greeks, Lebanese, Vietnamese and a huge number of Portuguese, which Mum couldn't pronounce—she'd always be saying things like 'I like these Pork and Cheese people'.

One day I had homework that required us to write down what we wanted to be when we grew up. The prime minister at the time was Bob Hawke, and Mum and Dad were always talking about him, grateful that he was personally allowing us to stay in *his* country. Every now and then we would say prayers, and after praying to God and Jesus and Mary we would offer thanks to Bob Hawke. I didn't even know what the word 'primeminister' meant, but I liked this guy whose job it was to allow people to live in his country and make them so happy.

One by one my teacher went around the classroom, and there were the usual firefighters, astronauts and all the Asian kids who had been told to say 'doctor'. I didn't once hear 'hot bread shop owner' or 'cab driver'. When it came to my turn I banged the desk and shouted 'primeminister'. It was a huge word for me and got me loads of kudos with the teacher.

I came home from school and over dinner told everyone about how I had declared today I was going to be primeminister. My mum's brothers didn't exactly laugh, but they ruffled my hair and said 'Of course you are', as if it was kind of cute—you know, like if a young Danny DeVito had said, 'I'm going to captain the LA Lakers'.

My uncles' reaction made my dad absolutely furious. I remember thinking, *He's overreacting a little bit isn't he?* But he was completely livid, laying into my uncles about their stupidity and how they were not to assume that his boy was as dumb as they were. As far as Dad was concerned, his kids ruled the world. At many a dinner party, my uncles would recall how on the boat trip Dad wouldn't let anyone touch the steering wheel, other than the designated drivers, and even threatened to throw people overboard if they did. But for long stretches of the voyage, he would hold me up to the wheel and let his two-year-old kid have a go.

Dad's enthusiastic, 'You can do anything' attitude, coupled with Mum's caring, 'Look after those less fortunate' approach, sounded like incredible advice to a kid, but I had to figure out the subtleties and deeper meaning of their advice. On more than one occasion I took them way too literally and found myself in trouble.

Sammy was a huge kid; the biggest kid in the year by a long way. He was mostly a grinning and laughing boy who liked to muck around and I never had a problem with him at all. We knew each other and at times even played in the same group. The only problem with Sammy was that he had an awful temper and every now and then something inside him would just snap and he'd explode.

One day we were playing handball and Sammy hit the ball over the line on the full. 'Out!' we all shouted. He refused to budge and so little Joey Santos pushed him off the court. We watched as the big fella turned around, grabbed Joey by the collar, and shaped up to belt him. Before I knew what I was doing, my hand shot out and grabbed Sammy's arm and suddenly I found myself in a fight with the biggest kid in Year 5. I can distinctly remember my mind saying to me, *Pull away. He's enormous.* But there was a louder voice in my head saying, *I can do anything. I can beat this guy.*

We traded punches for half a minute or so—*whack, whack, whack*—back and forth, and then it dawned on me that there was a searing pain in my cheek. I instinctively covered my head and stepped back, and the other boys rushed in to stop the fight. I got absolutely smashed. If it had gone on much longer he probably would've punched me all the way back to Vietnam. Sammy, of course, was completely unscathed.

I couldn't believe I'd lost. My dad's 'You can do anything' had settled in my little brain to such a degree that I was totally convinced

I was going to win. Instead, my first fight left me with a split lip, a bruised jaw and a battered self-belief. I went home that afternoon and lied: 'I ran into a guy when we were playing bull-rush.' That night, as Mum was tucking me into bed, she inspected my cuts.

'Does it hurt?'

'No', I said. She kissed me on the forehead.

'Tomorrow', she said, 'go up to the boy and make peace with him.'

The next day I went up to Sammy and was surprised when he threw a friendly smile at me. I smiled back and my lip split again. Over the coming months the strangest thing happened—Big Sammy and I became best friends.

One day we were the two last kids to get picked up from the front of school and I saw Sammy's father for the first time. Even just in the way his dad grabbed Sammy's bag, there was this pent-up aggression ready to go off. As they got to their old Kingswood in the car park, I heard a few loud words and then his dad started laying into him. Not like a measured smack on the bottom to reprimand a child, Sammy's dad was hitting him like an angry bar fighter trying to hurt a smaller opponent. Sammy wailed as he was almost thrown into the backseat of the car, and I quickly looked away as the car sped past, terrified his dad might've seen me witnessing something I should not have.

The next day I quietly went up to Sammy and asked him about footy cards, expecting him to talk to me about what had happened, but he never offered an explanation. It was never mentioned and I suspect it might not have been that rare an occurrence.

Soon after my family moved away from Marrickville and we had to say goodbye to Miss Buk. She gave us all hugs that lasted a little bit too long and were a little bit too tight, and then we all piled into our station wagon. As we pulled away she waved to us with one hand, the other trying to stop tears rolling down her face. Mum started sniffling as well.

'Such ungrateful children!' Mum was doing a great job of masking her sadness with anger, cursing Miss Buk's offspring for coming to see her so infrequently. In the years we lived in Marrickville, we only saw Miss Buk's children visit her maybe two or three times. Mum was desperately missing her own mother, who was a long way away in Vietnam, and couldn't comprehend why this lovely old lady's family, who only lived on the other side of Sydney, could let their mother be so sad and lonely.

We rented a two-bedroom house in nearby Earlwood. The house backed onto a park so Dad knocked off three fence palings and the park became our backyard. Three little kids went from a tiny apart-ment with no space to having what felt like the continent of Africa to play in. It was paradise. Beaman Park is enormous and has the Cooks River running through it, and Khoa and I spent our days wondering around, making up stories and exploring. Mum stayed home and looked after my baby sister, Tram, while Dad went to work in the factory.

One day, Mum's friend told her about how, with just a few hundred dollars, she had bought a second-hand sewing machine and could work from home while still looking after her kids. Of course, the following week there was an old, enormous industrial-sized Singer sitting in our living room.

Imagine something about the size of a V8 engine with a sewing needle and thread attached. Every time Mum pressed her foot on the pedal it would make an almighty roar. It sounded like we had a Kombi in our living room. A long *RAAARR* was the sleeve of the shirt, the cuffs were several short *RAR, RAR, RARs*, and a long

RAAARR again was up the other side of the sleeve. I would be glued to the TV watching *Happy Days* and just as the Fonz would say, 'Hey Ritchie, listen up, this is important. The secret to meeting girls is . . .' *RAARRRARRRRRARRRR*. I had little idea that this soundtrack was going to dominate my life for the next decade.

Mum and Dad discovered that working from home meant they didn't have to knock off at 6 p.m. They could keep going, and the harder they worked, the more money they made. All of a sudden their destiny was in their own hands. Dad left the job at the factory and started making clothes with Mum. It wasn't long before his entrepreneurial spirit and, you-can-do-anything attitude took over. He knew they were being paid peanuts by their employer, so they went to the source and got the work direct from the big wholesaler. Soon we had three uncles, four aunties and several distant cousins helping out, and we were running our own business.

My parents and their siblings worked and worked and worked. I look back now and the hours they did were absolutely ludicrous. But for a group of refugees who came from a communist regime where you had almost no means of making a living, they were in paradise. They were incredibly grateful they had the opportunity to be rewarded for their efforts, and worked accordingly. What a great country!

The business grew and so did the responsibility. There were days when the garments were running late and Mum and Dad would have to work through the night. Watching them work so hard, I decided to try to help and jumped on a machine to have a go. I had seen Mum do it a thousand times—*How hard could it be?*

I put a shirt sleeve under the needle and then stomped on the pedal. *RRRAAAAARRRRRRR!* The machine roared into action, sucked up three feet of material and my little seven-year-old left hand with it, neatly cross-stitching that soft bit of skin between the thumb and index finger to the cuff of a sky-blue business shirt. In seconds I had become a huge, kid-sized cufflink accessory, one that made a howling noise and bled everywhere.

I screamed a blood-curdling howl and ran around the house with the rapidly turning crimson shirt sewn to my hand, twice tripping over it. Mum came sprinting out of the kitchen and had to 'un-sew' a delirious, bawling child as my little brother and sister watched in open-mouthed horror.

After that incident my parents decided the best thing was not to ban the kids from the machines, but to actually teach us how they worked. To this day I am still an absolute gun at hemming, overlocking and buttonholing.

As the business grew, we moved again—this time to a factory in Newtown. Even back then, Newtown was the hippy capital of Sydney. It's actually a very cool place with lots of 'alternative types', people with multi-coloured hair, earrings through parts of their anatomy that aren't called an ear, and just general folk who love being different. But when you're an eleven-year-old kid walking to the station, a couple of guys with eyebrow studs, electric-blue hair and matching spiderweb tattoos down the left side of their faces are pretty frightening.

I was always on edge when we were at Newtown, but most of the time it turned out to be my own paranoia . . . those tattooed dudes mostly smiled and were harmless. The only time something creepy happened, we could not have seen it coming.

My brother and I were on the train one day heading to school. I was twelve and Khoa was ten. There was an old lady sitting across from us on the other side of the carriage. She kept looking at Khoa. Maybe she was thinking, *He's a bit fat for a Vietnamese kid*— because he was. Khoa was a chunky little fella who wore a school jacket that had been badly fixed up (*RRRRAAAAAARRRR!*) and which went down to his knees. So Khoa looked a bit odd and so people often stared at him, and I didn't think anything of it.

We arrived at our station and I saw this old lady get off also. I had never been so keen to get to school in my life. She followed us all the way—keeping about fifty feet behind us, but always watching—and stopped outside the school gates. At the end of the day, she was standing in exactly the same spot. She had waited outside our school all day! We rushed to the station and onto the train and she was nowhere to be seen.

'Thank God, she's gone now', I said to Khoa with relief.

We got off the train at Newtown and there she was, *again*. Now I was starting to freak out a bit. She kept her distance and followed us out of the station area, quietly shuffling along behind us, down all the streets we turned into. Khoa reckoned we should take a detour and go via the police station. I considered that option for a second and decided against it, reasoning that it would make the trip longer. I just wanted to be home as fast as possible.

As we turned into our street, we found ourselves walking faster and faster. We couldn't contain our fear any longer and we bolted home. We banged on the door and screamed, 'Open up. Open up!' My uncle let us in and we rushed upstairs and told our parents all about it.

My dad looked out the window and, sure enough, the old lady was hovering around on the street. She stayed for hours and hours. I begged my dad to call the police.

'What are you worried about?' he said.

'She's followed us since this morning', I pleaded with him.

'Just a homeless lady, she's harmless.'

'But she's probably crazy.'

Khoa joined my pleas: 'Yeah crazy. She's got this crazy look. I saw her look at me like she wants to eat me.'

I think, *Well, he is the fat one. That's how it worked with Hansel and Gretel.*

Then what Dad said next was odd, but really not surprising for him.

'You two go down and ask her what she wants.'

'What?!'

'She's harmless. Go down and see what she wants. I'll watch you from here.'

'What if she does something bad to us?' I asked.

'Like eats us', Khoa added.

'She can't do anything bad to you. Look at her. If she got into a fight with you two, who would win?'

'We would', Khoa said.

'Then you've got nothing to be worried about.'

And that was that. Khoa and I waited and waited at that window for another couple of hours and then the lady just tottered away. We never saw her again. That night at dinner my family talked about the whole encounter. Dad said:

'Always question your fear, Anh. There's almost never a good reason to be scared.'

My father hates fear.

The factory had a huge industrial space that Dad filled with V8 sewing machines, and offices which he turned into our make-shift home. I'm sure what he did was illegal—it didn't matter. No one knew, asked or cared. We lived there with Uncle Two's family. When we left Vietnam to come to Australia, Uncle Two left his family behind and came out on the boat with us (his family arrived later). Uncle Two was sickly as a child and out of all nine brothers he was the quietest, so Dad took it upon himself to look after his second eldest brother and had kept a close eye on him all his life.

What was fascinating about Uncle Two was his involvement in the war. This reserved and gentle man had a missing index finger on his left hand and if you asked him what happened he shrugged it off, and not tell you that he had spent a part of the war diffusing land-mines. One day he lost a finger, which he counted as an incredible blessing because most people in the same situation lost their lives.

These days mine diffusing is a much more scientific process, with engineers called 'sappers' being highly trained for the task. A while ago, I was watching TV and I saw footage of a mine diffuser strolling through a minefield in Afghanistan and I thought to myself, *This guy doesn't look all that nervous for a guy who's looking for landmines.* And then I realised he wasn't nervous because in front of him was a cameraman walking backwards.

My uncle was from the old school of sappers and he was somewhat of a hero in my father's eyes. With a thriving business, a huge factory and plenty of space, Dad invited Uncle Two and his family to move in with us. It was one of the best times of my childhood because Uncle Two had four sons around our age, and the whole bunch of us ran riot in this huge industrial space.

Khoa and I shared a bunk bed in an office, while my sister Tram slept in a bed in my parents' room, a converted dilapidated board-room. The old storeroom was shared by my uncle's four sons, Dung, Manh, Tri and Martin—yes, the youngest was called Martin; he was born in Australia. Eventually Dung, the eldest, who shared the same name as my Mum's brother, decided to change his name to Joe. A quick word of advice for any immigrants moving to a new country: before sending your children to school, please ask the immigration authorities if any of your names are a local word for 'poo'.

While they stayed with us, the boys went to our school and the six Dos made a funny looking group. At a sports event, the teacher lined us up and went through our names: Dung Do, Anh Do, Manh Do, Tri Do. He laughed and said, 'You guys are like a xylophone; Ding, dong, do . . .'

Even we had a giggle at that one.

Living with our cousins had massive advantages, but it also had one very embarrassing disadvantage.

One day at school the deputy principal knocked on my classroom door.

'Can I have a word with Anh when you have a moment?' he asked my teacher.

Stand back people, class captain business.

A couple of weeks earlier I had been voted class captain and even though I didn't know much about what it meant, my family made a huge deal of it and I was loving this newfound importance. I stood up and swaggered over to him like a Vegas nightclub singer. *Hey, thanks for coming, I'm here all week.*

Then, in front of the whole classroom, the deputy principal said to me, 'We're going to have to send you home because we've found nits on your cousin.'

C'mon man. You didn't have to say it in front of the whole classroom. I looked around and everyone had heard.

'Let's go, we've got to make sure it doesn't spread to the rest of the class. Grab your stuff.'

I made my way back to my desk and I've never seen ten-year-old kids move so fast. The thirty little rascals parted like the Red Sea, and there was me, little Vietnamese Moses with my head down and my cheeks bright red, walking through the middle, leading the nits to the Promised Land. I looked across and watched the girl I'd had a crush on for three years, little Alexandra, sliding behind Smelly Ross, using him like a human shield.

As I walked out I wouldn't have been surprised if they'd announced over the school PA system: 'Stand back children, poor immigrant coming through, make way for the lice-infested . . .'

Mum picked us up and bought the most toxic anti-nit lotion she could find. It stank, and hurt your eyes just to be near it. That afternoon six naked little Vietnamese boys were scrubbed with merciless brutality, like prisoners of war in a Da Nang concentration camp.

Our main living area in the factory was a space rather than a room, with dodgy furniture and a television in the corner. My father dumped a bed down to be used as a lounge and the six of us would lie on the bed, watch movies or World Championship Wrestling, and fall asleep on top of each other. Years later Mum would tell me she'd look at us and smile at the irony, here we were in Australia living in an enormously large warehouse, and still there's six kids sharing one bed—just like she did with her siblings back in Saigon.

Even though there were so many boys around all the time, my sister Tram was always looked after and never left out. My cousins, to their credit, gave her the first choice of lollies, or mangoes, or chocolates, even though she wasn't their sister. And in turn she looked after us. When you had six young boys running loose in a factory, there were always lots of bandaids to be put on.

One day, after we had gone to bed buzzing with adrenaline having watched *WrestleMania V* the night before, we were jumping around, acting like we were part of the Battle Royale. After eliminating Joe, Manh and Tri from the bed, I pinned down Khoa and was waiting for Tram—she was always the ref—to do the three counts. But, just like the real WWF refs, she was deliberately being cheeky and stalling on the third count. I thought the only way I was going to win was to toss Khoa off the bed. I'm pumped up and, not thinking straight, picked him up for an Ultimate Warrior throw. Then I chucked my younger brother straight onto a glass coffee table.

Amazingly the glass didn't break but two things were damaged: one of the table's wooden legs and Khoa's wrist. He let out a gigantic wail and we all freaked out, looking around to see if any adults were coming. In through the door walked my mum and we all breathed a sigh of relief—she was exactly the person you wanted to dish out the punishment.

One of the best things about my mum is her almost instant forgiveness. She never saw the point of punishment and as soon as she thought you saw the wrong in what you did, all was fine in her books. Whenever we got into trouble, even in a room full of adults, all us kids would turn straight to my mum and try and get her to be the person to punish us.

'Auntie Hien . . . we're so sorry, what must we do to make things better?'

Mum would say, 'Okay clean up your rooms'. When another parent tried to punish us more we'd protest: 'Auntie Hien has already punished us.'

We became very close to our cousins, they were like friends on tap. It was a charmed life for two years so we had no idea that it was going to end badly.

One day our cousin's mum came in screaming loudly, 'Which kid has taken my money!' She was missing a few hundred dollars from her purse and was incensed. Her kids weren't home, and so she turned on Khoa and me.

'Anh, was it you?' she accused aggressively. Then she turned to my brother.

'Khoa?' We both shook our heads.

'You better not lie! Who else could it have been?' She was really shouting now.

My mum heard the commotion and rushed in. She exploded at my auntie.

'Don't talk to my boys like that. They've never done anything like that and they never will.'

It was a clash of parenting styles, and was always going to lead to a blow-up. My mum is very much of the forgive-forgive-forgive, let-them-learn-from-their-mistakes school. Our cousin's mum was the keep-them-on-a-tight-leash type. As it turned out, there was no thief; one of her boys had taken the money and put it elsewhere for her husband.

There's always a big risk when you go into business with family or friends, and this is made even more intense when you all live together as well. A number of other events happened, one thing piling on top of another, and soon the two families went their separate ways. We did manage to salvage the relationship, however, and remained on speaking terms, seeing each other once in a blue moon, at Christmas and New Year's, but I missed my cousins very much.

Not long after Dad's brother Two moved out, his brother Three arrived from America and shacked up with us as well. Then a few months later, Dad's mum and little sister arrived from Vietnam and soon it was like that kid's song, but bigger: 'There were twenty-three in the bed, and the little Anh said 'Roll over, roll over'. So they all rolled over and Uncle Two moved out.'

Most of my childhood was like this; when Uncle Three returned to the United States, some of Mum's brothers lived with us, at other times there were distant relatives, or just people who needed a place to stay. Mum, especially, loved taking in people who were needy. I guess the one time nun-to-be never shook off her charity streak. Many of these people we would never see again once they moved on, but occasionally I am reminded of just how fascinating our childhood was.

About four years ago I was walking down the street when an old Vietnamese woman came up and hugged me.

'I haven't seen you for so long!' she squealed.

Who the hell is this? I asked myself during the sweaty bear hug.

'Your mum and dad took me in fifteen years ago. I cook for you, you love my fried rice, remember?' I smiled and nodded politely but I didn't have a clue. She could have been one of so many different people.

A lot of Vietnamese came out to Australia hopeful, but found themselves living in tough situations. Mum and Dad naturally seemed to attract these people. They radiated welcoming and compassionate warmth and people sensed it. My mother's active life within the Catholic Church also played a part. Word got around. My mother would hear about people with nowhere to go and simply say, 'Send them to me'. In turn, people would also talk about our family: 'Go to her, she will help you.'

In what was rapidly approaching a poker full-house, Uncle Six also lived with us for a while. Uncle Six was a big part of my childhood and what I remember about him most is that he had an enormous amount of empathy. Some might say this was because he was adopted and knew what it felt like to be an outsider, but I'd say he was just born this way.

I learned gentleness from Uncle Six. My father can be gentle when he wants to be, but mostly he doesn't. When I was nervous about my first-ever school camp in Year 3, Dad was away drinking, and it was Uncle Six who took me to buy a jacket—my first footy jacket; a Balmain Tigers beauty. I wore it like a black and orange safety blanket. Uncle Six showed me all the features of the jacket— pull-out hood, lots of pockets, even on the inside . . . like secret hiding spots. It had stuff to pull and tighten; all this was incredibly exciting for an eight-year-old boy. Having this wonderful new jacket with all its secrets somehow took away my fear, with my little brain thinking that if anything were to happen on this camp, my hood and six pockets were going to save the whole class. Well, as it turned out, my little classmates were soon going to have to save me.

All through my primary school years I had a thick Vietnamese accent: 'Fipteen minat twell equal tree'. Even though my English was getting better year by year, it was still definitely not as good as an Aussie kid's. It didn't seem to matter too much as I did well enough academically and socially, becoming a candidate for school captain at the end of Year 5.

There were four class captains in the running to become the big head honcho school captain. It was a very big deal, and the four of us were to make a speech in front of the whole school at the next assembly, to tell everyone why we were the best candidate for the job. The teacher pulled us aside and told us that it was okay to get help from our parents to write this speech, as it was such a big deal. I went home and said to Mum and Dad, 'You have to help me write a speech to become school captain'.

'Six! Anh needs your help to write his speech.'

Uncle Six had done a couple of years of school in Australia, and at the time he was the best at English in our whole household, but this didn't mean he was any good. Together we wrote my speech and on the day of the assembly I was ready to wow the school armed with a migrant's second-year English speech.

That morning I was first to speak.

'Hello School Peoples.'
'I am Anh.'

I could hear a few snickers from the other classes, but I was determined to go on.

'I will try for my hardest to be very friendly boy, and I will always saysing hello to all you school peoples . . .'

Everyone started laughing. The worst thing was when I looked down, I even saw teachers laughing. I looked across at my own teacher and she wasn't laughing, but I could see her trying not to laugh!

I was so mad at her. I froze. I didn't know what to do. It was almost like time stood still. In that moment I just totally blanked out and forgot what to say next.

The only people who weren't laughing were my little classmates. They were on my side. Just then I heard a tiny girl's voice:

'C'mon, Anh.'

I looked down and there was Karen, an 11-year-old face full of support. A few of her friends joined in.

'Keep going, Anh.'

'I . . . I . . . should be school captains because I want to helping the students . . .'

I stood as still as I could, just blanking out everyone, every noise, every snicker and laugh, and saying everything that I had to say like a monotone robot. Soon it was over. Thank God. My first ever public speaking experience.

I look back on it now and I can't even blame people for laughing. Bloody Uncle Six must've skipped the classes where they taught plurals and adjectives.

The boy and girl after me were much more polished and confident and then it was a boy named Edward's turn. The guy marched up with a clipboard like he's the governor-general or something and started reeling off words that made people go, 'Huh?'. And that was just the teachers. All us kids were sitting there with eyes glazed over, listening to a ten-minute routine that sounded like the prime minister's speechwriter was applying to get into Mensa. Little Tanya, one of my fellow candidates, turned to me and said, 'I don't care if I don't win, as long as this guy doesn't.'

It turned out Edward didn't win and I didn't either. It went to a tall kid named George who was a great choice. In all honesty I really didn't care, but a part of me wanted to do well because I knew my father was so excited about it. Throughout primary school I had won the odd academic award but it seemed like this pat on the back for leadership qualities meant much more.

Dad picked me up from school and, after I told him I didn't win, there was no change in his demeanour, he was just as exuberant. Maybe he knew it was always going to be a long shot. I'll never know, but he called up everyone to celebrate anyway. We all went out and had yum cha and it was one of the biggest celebrations I can remember in my childhood.

My brother was the biggest smartarse:

'As if they'd choose someone to be school captain who has nits.'

But my father treated that loss as if it were a win, and it was a lesson that stayed with me for a long time. If the worst happens, if you lose and fail, but you still celebrate coming second because you've given it a red hot go. There is no need to fear failure.

The following year, when I graduated Year 6, I was in the running to win the prize for maths. It was a big occasion in the school hall; we were all dressed up and everyone's parents were there. They announced third, then second, then finally . . .

'First: Anh Do!'

Sensational! I thought to myself. I got up to collect my award and as I made my way to the stage I looked back and saw my father get to his feet and give me a standing ovation. All by himself. Everyone saw him stand up and they probably thought he was going to look around, see that he was by himself and sit back down. But I knew better. Not my dad. I knew he didn't give two hoots what others thought, he was going to let his son know how overwhelmingly, beamingly, incredibly proud he was.

As I stood up on stage to have my photo taken, I looked down and thought to myself, *My dad's a legend.*

• Four •

I don't know if everyone has such fond memories of their first girl-friend, but every now and then when I hear a song by Milli Vanilli, like 'Blame it on the Rain', I'm reminded of my first love and waves of happy times come flooding back.

Her name was Karen. She was Vietnamese, ten months older than me, and half a foot taller. I didn't even know she liked me until the end of Year 5. On the last day of school kids used to bring presents for their best friends, and Karen walked up and gave me a little box with some small cakes of soap in the shape of a peach and a mango inside. I showed them to Uncle Six.

'I think she likes me', I said. He smiled.

'Maybe she thinks you need a bath.'

I was very slow when it came to the boy–girl thing. Then half-way through the holidays Karen invited me and a mate over to her house in the middle of the day. She had a friend there, too, a Portuguese girl named Elizabeth. Before you could say 'Pork and Cheese', we were playing spin the bottle. We weren't playing the naughty version, the one where you take your clothes off. It was the kissing variety: if the bottle spins to you, you had to kiss whoever it spins to next, unless they were the same sex, in which case you keep spinning.

I never knew the reason—maybe it was the dents in the carpet or the shape of the bottle, or maybe the gods of puppy love were just messing with my young head—but on this particular day

Elizabeth and I kissed eleven times and I didn't get my lips near Karen once. It didn't help that my mate, a chunky little guy called Peter with an even wobblier head than me, had got to kiss her about ten times. Karen was getting visibly more and more upset, and soon she began to try to manipulate the spin of the bottle. It bumped her outstretched foot and still bounced around to Peter. She coughed and her hand bumped it around for an extra spin, and back to Peter again. She wasn't happy and the penny *finally* dropped: *Wow, I think she really does like me!* Soon Karen got sick of her rotten luck and decided to fix things; after all, we were in her house.

'Stop the game!' she cried, and took me into the kitchen. She closed the door, and we pecked each other on the cheek—not on the lips. They were Karen's rules. We were very innocent. And that was it, I became her man and it was incredibly cool for a while. For a full six months, in fact . . . until a silly jump rope charity came to our school and tore us apart.

Jump Rope for Heart it was called, and all the school kids had to practise skipping so our families could sponsor us with a few dollars each, which went to a very worthwhile cause. For the ethnic boys who didn't have older sisters, it was the first time we'd ever tried skipping. It turned out, I was a natural. I grabbed each end of the rope, instinctively shuffled forward to get maximum swing, and *whoosh, whoosh, whoosh,* away I went.

I was no good at tunnel ball, hopeless at bullrush, and rubbish at all of those useful boy sports, but skipping was my forte. For a while it was great. I got a whole bunch of kudos for it, and it even momentarily made people forget the bad speech I'd given a couple of months before.

'Wow, look at Anh. He's a great skipper, who cares if he does speeches like an illegal Mexican.'

Karen loved it. Her man was the best male skipper in the class and she whisked me away from flicking footy cards with the boys to skipping with her friends. It wasn't too long, however, before she figured out that I had an even greater skill than skipping . . . holding the rope.

After two lunchtimes of being the 'rope boy' for a bunch of girls, while envying my mates belting each other at brandings with a bald tennis ball, I'd had enough. We broke up. Karen was my first girl-friend and I really was quite distraught when the whole thing ended. Again, it was Uncle Six who lent a sympathetic ear and helped me through it.

For a long time Uncle Six was like a surrogate father. I learned patience and temperance from him. It was a useful contrast to the bravado and impulsiveness of my dad.

Perhaps opposites do attract because Uncle Six got along with my dad really well. In fact, he was kind of like Dad's right-hand man. If Dad had a really important chore to be done, he knew he could rely on Six to accomplish the task.

One day, early on when the garment factory was flourishing, Dad was in Melbourne talking to the suppliers about extra units. He hadn't seen Khoa, Tram and I for a couple of weeks, and he missed us. Tram decided to stay home with Mum, but the two boys were trusted with Uncle Six and the van, which we stacked nearly to the brim with all sizes and colours of dressing gowns—a delivery for a Melbourne client. There must have been a couple of tonne of terry towelling in there.

Khoa and I crawled into the back cabin of the van and squeezed into the one-foot gap left between the top of the dressing gowns and the ceiling. It was just about the most comfortable, and fun, bed you could imagine. About four hours into the trip, we were zooming along on the highway when Khoa and I were awoken by a gigantic, very scary *BANG!* The van had careened out of control, and the two-tonne weight in the back was making it even harder to get it back on the straight. There was a screeching of tyres and then an abrupt *THUD!*

Uncle Six managed to keep his cool and carefully guided the van to the side of the road, stopping it safely by ramming it into a huge boulder. Khoa and I crawled out to see Uncle Six inspecting a blown-out tyre. We were in total darkness on a country road, and alone except for every once in a while when an enormous truck thundered past.

Uncle Six tried using the van's jack to lift the truck, but the sheer weight of the robes was too much. He tried a variety of different angles and positions for the jack, but it just would not budge. So he got down on his haunches, took a good look at the whole thing and went off into the bushes. He returned with a bunch of sticks and boulders and smaller wedge-shaped rocks and started placing them around the van in a strange manner, like he was going to start a religious ceremony or something.

He got Khoa and me to hold the steering wheel still while he used a huge branch to lever the boulder that had stopped us out of the way. With the help of gravity he pushed the van forward, making it mount a smaller rock and lifting the van just high enough for him to take off the tyre. Even to me, a little kid who knew nothing about physics or mechanics, it seemed like an incredible feat.

'How'd you learn how to do that?' I asked.

'Your father taught me.'

He replaced the tyre and about thirty minutes later we were on the road again.

We had a wonderful time on our visit to Melbourne. My father and uncle took us around to visit all the usual sights. As it was the first time Khoa and I had gone interstate, we returned with lots of gifts for Mum.

Then six months later, a strange thing happened. Uncle Six suddenly moved out and I never saw him again. He just disappeared. I asked Mum and Dad where he went, and they genuinely didn't know. One day he was my favourite uncle, the next day he was gone—no phone calls, no visits, no contact ever again. We didn't learn the truth until many, many years later; in fact, nearly two decades later.

In my last few years at primary school, Dad was talking about buying a farm. The sewing business had prospered, but he still had a hankering to reconnect with his family's farming roots, to go back to what he knew—the land and animals. So he found a duck farm, on seven acres of waterfront property at Swan Bay, two hours north of Sydney.

The farm was gorgeous, with a couple of houses on it as well as a swimming pool, but that was all window dressing to Dad. He saw the waterfront potential. Rather than just buying a cheaper block inland, he saw a chance to make some money out of breeding ducks, with a view to subdividing the land later.

The farm was beyond what Dad could afford but he wasn't one to let that stop him. Dad had a favourite Vietnamese saying that he always used to pull out, and it loosely translates as this: 'There's only two times in life, there's now and there's too late.' It goes a long way towards describing his outlook on life.

Dad roped in three of his brothers, Uncle Two, Uncle Three and Uncle Nine, who'd also come out from America. Together they bought the property and Two, Three, Four and Nine would rotate time spent there.

Dad had seen a niche market opportunity.

'Asians love duck eggs. If this goes well, I'll expand it', he told me.

He always had big plans for making big money. When I saw the farm, I had big plans for having a great time.

For two or so years, we visited the farm every school holidays and it was like the old days again because our four cousins who had lived with us in Newtown would come up as well. We'd all spend the holidays desperately searching for new and interesting ways to get into trouble. By this stage Joe was twelve, I was eleven, Manh was ten, Khoa was nine, Tri was eight, my sister Tram was seven, and their youngest brother Martin was kicking around our ankles. *Bang, bang, bang.* We were an assembly line, an indomitable force. Armed with spring rolls and duck eggs we would roam the surrounding marshlands for hours on end.

Dad bought a dinghy at an auction as well as a bunch of old oars, and we discovered the joys of fishing. One day Joe and I took the boat out by ourselves, just the two of us. Suddenly, I felt a huge tug on my line.

'Joe, I've got a big one!' The rod was bent like a banana, and I could actually feel it moving the boat along through the water. I thought it was going to pull me out of the boat so we panicked and cut the line. This left our boat rocking so hard we almost fell out.

'Ahhh!' Joe screamed and instantly turned white. I spun around and saw an enormous flipper not three feet away from our little dinghy. It slapped the water and rocked the boat again, forcing two terrified little boys to wail and cling on for dear life. Then this bald, leathery head slowly emerged from out of the water and an enormous eyeball stared straight at me for a second, then submerged.

It was a giant turtle, about five-foot long, with the most glorious and beautiful shell which gleamed in the sunlight. The turtle gave us a momentary display of its magnificence, then disappeared into the deep of the water again.

Joe and I rowed back to shore as fast as we could, in silence at first and then laughing hysterically, releasing the tension of the most terrifying thing we had ever encountered in our little lives—

apart from scary homeless women. As soon as we got back we told everyone about our ordeal, neglecting to mention the screaming, cowering or wailing like babies. Our fathers seemed proud that we'd survived a scare and got back safely. Later that week however, I got another scare that I wasn't meant to see, and it would change me forever.

Every morning at sunrise, our fathers knocked on our bedroom doors, and all six kids woke up, jumped into our gumboots lined up against the wall and went out to collect eggs. Free range, of course. Dad didn't like the idea of battery cages so nothing was too good for our ducks. They had an acre to walk around and Dad built sheds for them to lay their eggs in. If they didn't like it indoors, the ducks could waddle around under the trees surrounding them.

After a year, the ducks were producing great quantities of eggs and the farm was paying its way. The only problem with free range, Dad discovered, is that foxes could get to the ducks, so we went to the local pound and bought seven dogs.

Dad had an amazing knack of knowing which dogs were smart and could be trusted just by looking at them and playing with them for a few minutes. He really had a way with animals. He trained the dogs and they became an army of bodyguards for the ducks, and fantastic playmates for us. Not one fox got to the ducks after that, and we got to take the dogs fishing and exploring.

One rainy night we were watching TV when I looked out the back door and saw Blackie, a young kelpie cross, throwing up froth.

'Dad!' I yelled.

We all went out to inspect him and within minutes he was lying on his side whimpering, unable to even move. Some people had gone fishing at a local bay, caught a couple of poisonous toadfish and irresponsibly left them lying around on the shore. All the dogs knew to avoid the toadfish but Blackie was young and naive, and he'd swallowed a deadly carcass.

Dad got me to call up the local vet, which was a good forty-minute drive away, but it was closed. Dad told Joe and me to keep the kids occupied, away from the back door. Once Joe had the others entertained, I snuck back out and saw my father tenderly carry Blackie in his arms like a small child to the side of the shed. Then he picked up a huge shovel, lifted it high above his head and . . . *wham!*

It was over. A single blow.

Dad silently used the same shovel to bury the dog in the rain, like a scene in a Stephen King movie. Mum came over and put her arm around me when she saw that I was watching through tears of sadness and frustration. I was only eleven years old and I didn't understand the idea of 'putting it out of its misery'.

'Why did he do that? What if Blackie got better in the morning?' I argued with Mum. She gently explained that it would have been cruel to let him suffer in agony all night, that Blackie was well past gone, and what Dad did was actually the kind thing to do.

'Your father loved Blackie, too, Anh. But he knows when an animal is near its end.'

The next morning all of us kids went out and made a cross out of sticks and Tram picked some flowers that we quietly laid under the tree next to the shed where little Blackie was buried. It didn't matter that it was only a dog, or that we had six others. We were kids who had just experienced our first death of a pet.

I adored the farm. My favourite childhood memories are of being there and playing around, and also of how Mum and Dad were so in love with each other when we were there. Mum was so proud when Dad and his trained dogs caught the fox that was eating our ducks.

'Your father's the best when it comes to animals', she would say to no one in particular.

It seemed like my parents were in their element. This rural-raised couple from a third-world country were at peace on the land.

In the evenings we would all sit down in front of our little TV and watch *MacGyver*. He was awesome; he could turn a can of tuna and a pocket torch into an alternator and save a planeload of Colombians. Dad would always sit back and treat the show like a challenge, commentating on what might realistically work and what would not. Sometimes he would predict what Mac was going to do next. 'Wow!' All us kids would be mesmerised as we watched Dad's prediction unfold, but Mum was never surprised. She knew what her man was capable of and, in her mind, no *MacGyver* stunt was ever going to top how her young husband had single-handedly gotten her brothers out of a concentration camp.

I also loved it when Dad taught me things. I felt so privileged to be learning the secrets only a chosen few would ever know. One time my uncle locked his car keys in his old Toyota and Dad went and fetched a coat hanger. He bent it out of shape and then, within a few minutes, *click*, the car was unlocked. Everyone was impressed, smiling and relieved . . . for a few short seconds. Dad immediately locked it again and slammed the door shut.

'Anh! Your turn.'

He threw me the crooked coat hanger and went back inside to finish his beer with my uncle.

My brother and I worked hungrily on the lock. We had just seen Dad do it and here was our chance to perform a feat that felt like a magic trick, or at the very least part of a spy's arsenal of skills. A couple of times I could see the lock ever . . . so . . . slowly . . . rising . . . then, before I could lift it all the way up, it'd slip and fall again.

After an hour, just as I was about to give up... *click!*

Whoo-hoo!

It's hard to describe how satisfying it was. I once spent two hours with a mate throwing basketballs at the ring from the halfway line. After a few hundred attempts, *thwip*—straight through! That's what it felt like.

I ran inside, yelling, 'I done it! I done it!'

Picking a car lock is a bit like riding a bike, once you've done it, it kind of stays with you forever. As I got older it became very handy. At university I was the go-to man for girls who'd locked their keys in their car: 'Yes, ma'am, I'm happy to help'. I used to go to parties hoping someone would forget their keys in the car just so I could be the hero. On the school bus I'd daydream about everything from a hijacking to a thermonuclear war, all I'd have to do is reach into my schoolbag and pull out my trusty coat hanger.

Dad was always building a shed, mending a fence or making an enclosure.

'Can we keep some budgies?' we asked him one day.

'Okay', he said, 'but you've got to build the cage yourselves.'

This was Dad's way of training us to learn practical skills; he was very hands-on. He took all of us to town to buy the wire. The only car we had up at the farm was the work van which had a bench in the front and no seats in the back. The two youngest kids, my sister and Martin, sat next to Dad in the front; us five other boys sat on the floor of the van in the back. Every time it turned a corner, we'd all *whoop* with delight.

'Turn again, Dad', I pleaded. 'Come on, swoosh us around.' It was totally illegal and totally fantastic. We would sit on the wheel hub on the floor and start hanging on to it as we wound our way around the country roads. For twenty minutes it was great fun, but after that the floor started getting hot because it was right above the engine. Soon our arses could stand the heat no longer and we would have to jockey around for a cooler position.

After we bought the wire, Dad sat us down in front of his duck enclosure.

'Right, have a look at this.' We inspected it.

'Based on that, work out how you might build a smaller cage for budgies.'

So the six of us boys went to work with saws and pliers, and Tram had her busiest day ever with the bandaids. Eventually we finished a cage that was wonky, not quite square, but to us it looked like a bird Taj Mahal. It passed Dad's inspection and we headed off to buy some budgies.

I love auctions. I love the discovery part of them. Often you turn up not knowing what you might find and it's like unearthing treasure. Then you try and anticipate what things might sell for, hoping no one else wants that American Indian with the flashing neon eyes, and get worried when a rich-looking old lady starts inspecting it closely.

My dad used to take us to livestock auctions. We'd roll up in the van, get out and discover a zoo of fascinating beasts. Except with this zoo you get to buy the animals and take them home. *Brilliant!*

Ferrets, puppies, budgies, goats, parrots, ponies—for an eleven-year-old kid it was magic. What made it even more exciting was going with a nutty impulsive dad, who would actually buy stuff you asked for. You didn't always get what you wanted, but my dad was the type of guy you could try it on.

'Dad, how about a little guinea pig?'

'Nah, looks like an overweight rat with its tail bitten off.'

We once rolled up to an auction and there were these funny creatures that looked like miniature camels. Dad had never seen anything like them before in his life. Not even in photographs.

'What the hell's that?' he asked.

'They're called alpacas, Dad. We learned about them at school last year. They're good for wool.'

'They're funny looking, aye. What do they eat?'

'I think they eat grass. Like sheep but different.'

'Eight!' He squeaked. 'Check out these things. They keep the grass low, Anh reckons.'

'Chuck 'em in the back paddock if they go cheap', Uncle Eight suggested. I waited the rest of the afternoon in painful anticipation.

'Lot number 157—chooks . . . number 162—rabbits . . . 164—goldfish.'

C'mon, c'mon, just get to the alpacas already.

'Lot number 241—a pair of Peruvian alpacas.'

It was intense and exciting and I don't remember much except that I watched as the price got to my dad's set maximum and he stopped bidding.

There's still a chance, I thought. Every now and then Dad would stop at his maximum but then, just as the auctioneer was about to bang the gavel for the third time, Dad would stick up his hand and try to give the guy a wrist sprain from stopping too suddenly. I was hoping that would be the case this time.

'Sold! To green shirt at the back.'

Damn. We missed out.

'Next up, lot number 242—a male golden pheasant.'

The thing about Dad, the next auction immediately after he loses an auction is a very good time to get him to buy something.

'Dad! Can we have a pheasant? Pheasant's are good for long grass too!'

Dad loved birds—ducks, chickens, sparrows and even those annoying myna birds. He reckoned that in Vietnam he knew a kid who taught one to say, '*Da Dao thang Viet Cong Hoi*'. ('Piss off, you smelly Vietcong.') I never believed him until I got older and an

Indian mate told me that in his country mynas are like cockatoos. So Dad was interested in the pheasant.

'Beautiful feathers . . . like a yellow peacock', he said.

That afternoon, when Mum heard the van come up the driveway, she wondered, *What useless animal did he buy this time?*

In we walked with our pheasant.

'Oh my god. What are we going to do with that?' she asked.

'Forty-five bucks! Beautiful isn't it? We'll keep it in the backyard', Dad replied. He paused for a second, then added, 'And if it doesn't work out, we'll cook it'.

One day my dad was driving around and saw some feed for sale by the side of the road. It wasn't just a bargain, it was the bargain of the year. 'So cheap, have to buy it.'

Dad bought a small amount, just to see if it was okay, because sometimes cheap feed can be off. The ducks loved it. Dad was excited. The next day he sent Uncle Nine back to buy a dozen bags, enough to feed the whole farm that afternoon.

The next morning we woke up to find several thousand dead ducks. The feed was dodgy—the trial sample had been random luck.

That was the end of the farm, and that was the end of my dad the farmer. It all went downhill after that. He and his brothers held on to the property for a while, and thought about buying more ducks. 'Otherwise, what the hell do we do with it?' he asked.

Before anyone could give him a considered answer, the property bubble burst. It was 1989, interest rates hit eighteen per cent, and the farm was sold for a loss. Mum and Dad went back to scrounging out a living sewing clothes in our living room.

• Five •

For a large part of my childhood my dad's mum lived with us. We called her *Ba Noi*, which is Vietnamese for paternal grandmother. She was an important part of my upbringing as most of the time it was her who looked after us while Mum and Dad were busy sewing.

Grandma loved gardening. Every house we lived in that had a backyard would be turned into a Saigon paddy with eggplants, snakebeans, basil, Vietnamese mint, melons and limes. Grandma knew exactly which plants needed chicken wire put around them to fend off Dad's dozen or so ducks and the golden pheasant, which he'd named 'Dinner'. Our front yard would be filled with flowers and bright orange cumquat trees laden with fruit. Old Aussie ladies would see Grandma in the front yard tending this exceptional flora display and ask her questions. She would happily turn to them and flash her black-toothed smile, which probably freaked them out.

Grandma always had a wonderful youthfulness about her. She used to come in after a hard day's work in the garden, crack open a can of VB, put her feet up and sing karaoke. At the time I owned a Nintendo game console and one of the earliest versions of a shooting game. You sat back three or four metres from the TV, pointed the laser gun at the screen and shot the animals that flew past. I spent a full year perfecting my aim and I had just managed to crack the game and make it to the end.

The very day after I finally did this, I woke up at midnight and heard the *doo-doo-loo-whoop* of someone breezing through the game, scoring hit after hit after hit. I came out to the living room to see Grandma, who had been having bouts of insomnia, plonked on two Yellow Pages phone books in front of the TV, shooting away. She literally had the laser gun touching the screen. *How could she miss?*

I glanced at the score and realised she was only two levels away from the end that had taken me a year to reach! I had to sit next to her and cheer her on as she finished the game like I had the night before. The next morning I told everyone about it and my brother and sister wanted to see. Grandma was so proud of herself that she stacked the two phone books in front of the TV, and did it all over again while we had breakfast.

Having a cool grandma living with you was wonderful thing, but like with all the elderly, there were a few rules you had to follow. The first was: 'Never leave important paperwork lying around just in case it ends up in the bin'.

One day I came home from school and Mum asked me to retrieve my Australian citizenship certificate as we were applying for something important. After I found it, Mum told me to put it away in a safe place because I had to take it to school the next day. One of my favourite television shows was about to start, so I left it on the kitchen bench.

'Where's the form?' Mum asked me the next morning when it was time to leave for school. I couldn't find it. Two hours later we'd turned the house upside down and we still hadn't found it.

'Go outside and check in the bin', my mother said. 'Might as well have a look in there.'

I went and pulled out last night's rubbish. A surge of excitement and relief flooded through me as I glimpsed the certificate's creamy colour. I pulled out my citizenship certificate and un-scrunched it, finding three snapper heads wrapped up inside.

Grandma couldn't read English so she had no idea what she'd done, and I'd left the certificate lying among some Kmart pamphlets, which she thought were perfect for wrapping up fish heads. I headed off to school extremely late and carrying a schoolbag that smelt like the back alley of the fish markets. I avoided a clout on the head for that one but only just.

My family were, and still are, extremely paranoid when it comes to documentation. That night at dinner one of my uncles summed up the fear: 'If you don't have your identity papers they'll kick you out of the country'. In hindsight I can see where their fear came from. Those pieces of paper meant we were safe and without them my family felt as vulnerable as someone selling snacks on a Saigon train with no permit.

My parents always believed in giving us kids as good an education as they could afford. So when it was time for me to go to high school they searched high and low for the best school.

Uncle Huy, who was in training to become a Jesuit priest, was somewhat of an expert on schools. He had travelled around, written references for families trying to get their kids into the best Catholic colleges, and even done a bit of teaching here and there.

'You've got to send the boys to St Aloysius', he said to my parents. 'It's the one. It's got great academic grades but it also teaches them how to live a great life.'

When Mum and Dad looked into it they were sold. The school had two mottos. First: 'Men for Others'—done deal as far as Mum was concerned. Here was a school that was going to teach her boys to look after others and, if she hadn't drummed it into us enough at home, we'd get another dose at school. The other motto was: 'Born for Greater Things'. *Boom*! Dad's happy.

'Now *that's* a school motto', he said. 'None of this, 'We'll try our hardest blah blah blah' crap. Born for Greater Things! That's the school for my boys! How much is it?'

When the lady told him the fees, he turned to Mum and said in Vietnamese, 'Holy Schmoly . . . Born for expensive things!'

Khoa and I giggled.

'No problem!' he said. He'd decided then and there that he was going to do whatever it took to pay those big fees.

As we drove home I listened to my parents discuss how they were going to afford it, the plans they would put in place, the different strategies and sacrifices. In that moment, my naive little brain realised something big about Mum and Dad. All the effort, all the late nights sewing till 3 a.m., all the risks to get us onto a boat and take on the ocean was for one reason: so that they could give their children a better life.

When we got home we flicked through all the pamphlets the school had given us and we found a page that had a magic word on it: Scholarship.

'Woo-hoo!!!' says Mum. It was like she had opened the pamphlet and out fell a scratchie with three matching horseshoes on it.

'Anh! Khoa! All you got to do is sit a test and ace it, and you get to go to the school for FREEEEE!' Her voice lifted to a grand crescendo at the end and Khoa and I tried to calm her down.

'You gotta win it first, Mum. Like, probably thousands of kids go for it, and they've only got a few.'

'You'll win it', she said.

'What if we don't?'

'Doesn't matter.' I love how Mum always said 'doesn't matter'. Not even a loaded 'doesn't matter', like a 'it *really does matter* and your mum will be devastated if you don't do this for her', but a real honest-to-god 'doesn't matter'. It was like when I had to do that speech to become primary school captain: 'Doesn't matter'.

I guess when you'd been shot at by pirates and faced starvation on a leaky boat, these little things really do seem trivial. That's one of the most astonishing things about both my mum and dad. They always had mammoth dreams for us, but at the same time they never put us under any pressure.

They also seemed to have a different reaction to failure. Dad especially was always positive, even a little bit over the top when we failed. 'Great, son! At least you know you're sailing near the edge of your capacity!' It was a strange concept for a kid to wrap his head around.

Armed with the knowledge that your parents had full belief in you, but yet wouldn't be at all fazed if things didn't work out, Khoa and I attended those exams and we both ended up winning partial scholarships. It wasn't the big one where you get to go totally for free, but Mum and Dad only had to pay half the fees.

'Wonderful! Wonderful! Wonderful!' Mum shrieked. And we were off for a McDonald's Happy Meal to celebrate. It was the last McDonald's outing we had as a family because things were about to take a turn for the worst.

• Six •

My father is an eternal, incurable optimist. He has this incredible combination of self-belief, mixed with an addiction to risk taking:'You can do anything', 'There's now and there's too late'. But for a period back then it seemed like the universe was conspiring to break him because it hit him with wave after wave after wave of misfortune.

When the farm was prospering Dad and his brothers had invested in a number of properties: a huge three-storey factory in Leichhardt, a house in south-western Sydney, as well as another block of rural land. Soon after the heartbreaking events at the farm and the onset of high interest rates, there was simply no way he and his brothers could afford the inflated repayments. They hung on for as long as they could and then eventually sold everything at a massive loss. So Dad not only lost his own money but all the savings of his brothers as well.

Now Dad's the type of guy who can bounce back after a financial setback, but losing the trust and friendship of his brothers was crippling for him. One night I awoke to the most awful sounds of swearing, breaking furniture and bodies thumping against the wall. I ran out to see my father and Uncle Three tangled in a bloody wrestle on the floor of our living room. They were trying to kill each other. My mum was screaming for them to stop, threatening to call the police and at the same time trying to shoo away the kids from the appalling scene.

I ran back into my room and tried my best to block out the dreadful noise. For the first time in my life I was genuinely afraid.

My father eventually got in the car and left. Where he went I don't know but he returned the next day. Shortly after that Uncle Three moved out and returned to America.

Dad then went into a downward spiral. He'd always been a pretty heavy drinker but now he began drinking copiously, and it wasn't until many years later that my mother explained to me the depth of my father's guilt.

Uncle Three left Vietnam on a boat about six months before we made our journey. He had with him three brothers: uncles Five, Seven and Nine. Just like our boat, they were attacked by pirates. Unlike on our boat, there were very few survivors. After the pirates took everything they sank the boat in the middle of the ocean, and the 32 people on board were forced to cling onto bits of debris at the mercy of the raging Indian Ocean.

Uncle Three passed out and woke up on a beach in Malaysia. After searching desperately for other survivors he found Uncle Nine alive. Eventually they found the dead bodies of uncles Five and Seven. When news got back to Vietnam that two brothers had died on the trip my father blamed himself for not being on the boat.

For a while there had been talk of Dad and our family joining that earlier boat but we eventually stayed to await another journey. My father felt that he might have been able to do something to save his brothers had he been with them. Although he was technically brother number Four, he was always a leader among his siblings.

When uncles Three and Nine joined Dad in Australia it was clearly obvious how much they meant to him and how much he wanted to make their lives better after them having endured the tragedy of finding two brothers' tattered bodies sprawled out on the rocks. Now he had somehow managed to lose all their money, and the guilt ate away at him.

He felt guilty not only about uncles Three and Nine, but Uncle Three's wife as well. While searching for other survivors from their boat, Uncle Three saw a person struggling out at sea. He swam out and saved the life of a young lady. The two became friends and eventually married. This couple had endured enough. Now, after a stint in Australia where they had worked hard and eventually made some progress, they were returning to the United States with absolutely nothing.

'Is that why he feels guilty, Mum?' I asked.

'That's a part of it, but not the biggest part of it. Your father blames himself for the death of his eldest brother.'

Dad's drinking was getting out of hand and he was no longer holding down a job, or helping out with making the garments. He was turning into a regular drunk and the tipping point for Mum was when he turned violent.

About half a dozen times when I was a young teenager my father hit me in a drunken stupor, without measure, without controlled words of admonishment to soothe the wounds, but wildly and with intent to cause pain, like Sammy's dad. Well, when you teach your son that he can do anything, you shouldn't be surprised if he hits you back. On what was to be the last occasion I flung myself in Dad's direction and pushed him into the wall, smacking my fist into the side of his head. I cried and screamed at the same time, I was delirious. My defiance struck him harder than my fist ever could. It shocked him and he stumbled away in confusion.

Dad often seemed to disappear for weeks on end and then one day Mum told us that he had gone back to Vietnam for a while.

'What's a while, Mum?' I asked.

'I'm not sure, maybe a year.'

Ahhh, relief, I remember thinking to myself. *No drunk in the house for a year.*

We didn't see my dad for about six months and then one day my mother announced, 'I have just heard that your dad is back in the country. I have told him I don't want to see him again. I can't have him being violent towards you kids.'

I didn't say anything. The penny dropped. I understood. Instinctively, I steeled myself to protect Mum and my siblings from my father's potential response to this act of rejection. I found myself lying awake in bed at night, thinking about how I would defend my family.

If he lays a finger on Mum, I will kill him, I said to myself. I took the largest kitchen knife I could find and stuck it under my bed. I was thirteen and at least as heavy as my dad, if not as tall. I figured I might stand a chance if I had a weapon.

It's hard to describe how strange it feels when you cross that line. When you break through having a fear of your father and decide that you're ready and willing to hurt him. Fear and adrenaline mix like a bubbling poison that eventually explodes and you find yourself scarred and distorted, and you can never go back. You lose respect for him, for authority in general. Then all the things that he represents, all the principles, start to crumble and you ultimately lose respect for yourself.

One night my mum came into my bedroom. The terror on her face was obvious—she was as pale as a sheet and had been crying.

'Your father's coming.'

I locked up my little brother and sister in the toilet and answered the door. A drunken man stood in front of me.

'Where's your mum?'

'Inside.'

'Get her out here.'

'No.' *No, you stupid fool. You no longer have the right to order anyone around. And if you try and force your way in, I will kill you.*

My mum came running out.

'What do you want?' she asked him through tears. She pushed me back and even through her palpable terror she put herself in a position to defend me. I went back inside to get my knife.

I returned to the door and my father was sobbing. I was shocked. I had never seen him like this before. Ever. He turned and walked away, and I didn't see him again for the rest of my childhood.

• Seven •

St Aloysius was a great school. But what caused a lot of discomfort for Khoa and I was the socio-economic mismatch of private school expenses versus our single mum's wages. We were on half scholarships, which helped, but even with fifty per cent off the fees, it was a massive struggle.

Mum found it difficult to buy a jacket that fitted Khoa, who was a big and overweight kid at sixty kilograms when we first started at the school. He was short and stumpy, so a jacket that fitted his shoulders and back would have sleeves that were way too long. As alterations were expensive, Mum worked out a cheap solution: she simply lopped off the ten centimetres of excess sleeve.

During the six years I spent at St Aloysius I never quite had the right fitting uniform either. In Year 7 Mum bought me a jacket that was a little bit bigger to make sure it would last as long as possible. It lasted me till Year 9. By Year 10 the jacket was too small. Khoa's old jacket fitted me perfectly around the body, but the sleeves only went halfway down my forearms! As Mum had thrown out the original material three years earlier she searched high and low at every fabric shop from Marrickville to Bankstown, but just couldn't find a match for the grey of the jacket. So she bought the closest grey possible and used it to lengthen my sleeves. I walked around with a jacket that was one colour of grey down to just past the elbow, and then a totally different shade of grey to the cuffs. Being a boy's school

I don't think the other kids ever noticed, but that didn't mean I wasn't paranoid about it.

I remember one time I won a prize at Year 10 graduation, which was a big deal held at the Sydney Town Hall. I felt dread when I heard my name called out because it meant getting up and standing on stage in front of the whole school. In my mind I could hear them all saying: *Jesus, look at that jacket, it's two different colours. For god's sake, how poor are that family?*

While up on stage I crossed my arms and made a mental note to self: Next year, you idiot, do well, but not so well you have to get up in this stupid jacket.

Then there were the other uniforms we needed, all of it top-of-the-range high-quality stuff, all of it very, very expensive. The St Aloysius winter catalogue makes the latest Gucci release seem limited. The sports uniform is different to the PE gear, which changes each semester, and is different again to the rugby gear, and the soccer, cricket and basketball outfits. Add to this the fact that sport is compulsory in both summer and winter, and you have a very large uniform bill for two relentlessly growing teenage boys.

Mum had another brilliant solution. She would scour St Vinnies and other op shops for items that looked similar and then just cut off the St Aloysius badges from our old stuff and stick them on the 'new'. *Voila!* If you panned a video camera along the Under 15A rugby side warming up you'd see a consistent royal blue all the way across until you got to me. My jersey was more a faded cobalt, like someone had hung me on the washing line for three months and forgotten I was there.

Many people ask me after a comedy show: 'Were you the class clown?' I was nowhere near so. In fact, I was at the other end of the spectrum: a quiet kid who was studious and focussed on my work.

In Year 7 every kid in the form did a subject called drama, which was just about everyone's favourite because it was basically mucking around, play-acting and putting on little shows. It was a glorious break from the boredom of maths and chemistry, and I loved it. It was also a break from real life when your life was full of worries and concerns. My mind was always chattering and churning out the same thoughts: *Will they see my two-toned jacket? Mum's sick again. I don't have the money for next week's excursion.* In drama, all of a sudden, you could stride into a battle scene wearing a helmet and vest, reciting heroic lines that save the kingdom. Instantly your worries would fade away.

For that brief double period of make-believe you got to float away on an intoxicating bubble of imagination. You got to escape into a fantastical world where you could experience the highest highs and the lowest lows, death, love, betrayal, winning the princess, killing the villain, even being the villain. And yet no one could be harmed, the dead brother returned to being your best mate, Phil, and you all have a laugh at how Phil took so long to die.

Then in Year 8, the school did a weird thing. It decided that half of the class would get to do drama and the other half would never have any potential.

So at the beginning of Year 8, Mr Stevens, the drama teacher, walked in and ran a ten-minute exercise—which was some sort of theatre game—and then proceeded to pick the fifteen deserving boys and cull the fifteen no hopers.

When Mr Stevens started to assemble his star class we all sat there in anticipation. I reckoned I had a pretty good chance because the year before I had done well at the subject. It was like those horrible times in the playground when two captains get to pick their teams and your self-esteem endures a knife wound with every kid picked before you. You look around and hope that you're not stuck at the end with the nerd and the fat kid. Then the end arrives and you're the very last one standing, and you realise with abject misery that you are the nerd *and* the fat kid all rolled into one.

As I watched Mr Stevens select his fifteen stars, I started to get worried about a trend that was emerging. He was basically picking the loudest boys in the class—all the class clowns, the ADHDs, the look-at-me-I-need-to-be-noticed types. I was thinking, *Oh man, there's a real chance I might miss out here.* There was so much tension in the room; *A Dancing with the Stars* elimination is nothing next to this.

I counted the grinning faces on the other side of the room, noting there were twelve already. I looked left and right at the bunch of remaining rejects and, sure enough, we were the quieter ones.

What an idiot, I thought. *There's still a bunch of great talent sitting here. C'mon, don't you realise some of the world's best actors were introverts: James Dean, Robert De Niro, Charlie Chaplin . . . C'mon!*

Three more places left and he called out the names.

Not me . . . damn!

Not me . . . damn!

Not me, again. Bloody hell. My heart sank.

I rationalised that I wasn't really the performing type. I'd *rather* sit in a room and stare at the clock, waiting for the talented boys to come back and tell me all about their heroic adventures. And that's just what I did. For many, many long periods.

Then one day Mrs Borny, our English teacher, who I've always thought was my very own real-life version of Robin Williams' character in *Dead Poets Society*, walked in and decided that us bunch of rejects weren't hopeless and started to run her own drama classes. She had never agreed with splitting up the class in the first place, and even though she'd never taught drama before, she improvised and pretty soon we were doing our own version of plays and acting games. Suddenly this bunch of rejects felt like the lucky ones, the ones taught by 'The Secret Drama Teacher'.

Mrs Borny not only taught us drama but also how to write it, creating stories from scratch. One day she said to me, 'Anh, you're a very talented storyteller'. She had no idea how far that one line of encouragement would take me ... until twenty years later, when this little boy became a famous comedian and surprised her on a TV show called *Thank You*.

It's funny how boys and girls are treated differently. My sister always got a haircut at the hairdressers but Khoa and me, that was a job for Mum. And she was appalling at it. No training, no method, no tools; just a pair of kitchen scissors—the type that you use to cut chickens apart—and a two-buck comb. She always took it slowly, figuring she wouldn't start too short and give herself room for error, and then she would slowly chip away at it until it kind of looked right. But it never looked right.

One side too short, a patch missing, a crooked fringe. It looked so bad that when I went to school the next day all my friends thought I had picked up some sort of disease. A couple of mates waited until we were alone and asked, 'What happened there?' It looked so bad that no one even laughed; they really thought something bad had happened.

'I got into a fight a few years back', I'd lie. 'There's a scar, and a bit less hair there.' They believed it.

Once, as soon as I had a spare fifteen bucks, I took myself to the barber. When I walked in, the Indian guy dropped his Brylcreem and shrieked,

'Oh my god! What in the name of Vishnu happened to you?'

Even a professional was fooled into thinking there was something physically wrong because of the accidental brutality of my mother's efforts.

Later a friend of Mum's came over and saw my wobbly head.

'Get yourself a pair of clippers', she advised Mum. 'Use a number three setting all over, all the time, and you'll be fine.'

Mum bought a pair of twenty-dollar Kmart specials. They lasted a few years. They used to jam up because they were cheap, and I had thick hair. Mum would yank them out—and I'd get clumps of bald spots. As it grew back it evolved into another look altogether. You know, when you sleep on the one side for too long and the next day your hair decides to tell the world which side you prefer. Well my head looked like that permanently.

I was also starting to look a lot like my dad.

When times were good Mum and Dad used to take us to McDonald's once every few months. Usually for a special occasion like Christmas, or Khoa winning a scholarship, or Dad's horses coming in at the races. It signalled good times and, even today, when I bite into a Big Mac and get a hit of that 'special sauce', I get a dose of memories flooding back.

In 1993 Mum was working multiple jobs to feed three teenage kids. Rice is cheap, but combined with chicken thigh or drumsticks at $5 a kilogram, well, you've got a few days' worth of meals. We hadn't been to McDonald's in years. I came home from school one day, lifted open the letterbox and discovered a flyer announcing 'McDonalds Yagoona is closing down'. Because it was the first-ever Maccas to open in Australia, to commemorate its last day there was going to be a never-seen-before special. It read: 'bring this flyer in and get a Big Mac for fifty cents'.

Fifty cents! Whoo-hoooo!!!!!

'Limit four per voucher. One voucher per customer.'

No problem. I knocked on the door of my closest neighbours and asked them if I could have their Maccas flyer if they weren't going to use it. I managed to get six vouchers altogether. That would be a whopping twenty-four Big Macs.

Mum, Grandma, Khoa, Tram and I packed into our car—we must have looked like a Vietnamese version of *The Beverley Hillbillies*. Five vouchers used up. We drove around the block, dropped off my grandma and picked up my auntie to take advantage of the sixth voucher. With twenty-four Big Macs in tow we headed home with guilty grins on our faces. Still today my brother and sister talk fondly of the Big Mac banquet we enjoyed; our enthusiasm rivalling those of our uncles when they talk of their great plum banquet during the war.

Then there was that day I scored on chips. I'm one of those guys who likes to read things. Anything. The paper, road signs, even the back of a packet of chips. So I knew that if you were ever unsatisfied with a chip there was a number you could call. Well one day I was halfway through a packet of potato crisps when I found a green chip, so I called them up.

'Send the offending chip to us and we'll pay for the postage', the woman on the phone told me, 'and we'll refund your money'.

The packet of chips was only a couple of bucks but I reasoned that the refund would at least be enough for me to buy another packet. I sent off the green chip straight away and didn't really think about it too much. A week later, a humungous box of chips was delivered to my door. There must have been thirty packets inside. It felt like Christmas.

For a week I had the same chips as everybody else at school instead of the no frills variety that I used to eat really fast so I could quickly dispose of the black and white bag. I sauntered out at recess with my big packet of branded chips and ate them proudly in front of the other boys, offering them to friends like I was all cashed up. For a week I was normal.

These little windfalls of luck meant so much to us; to go from having to scrape by to all of a sudden having something in abundance made such an impression. I often ask my mum about Vietnam, what it was like being in the middle of a war, and her answers would sometimes surprise me. She told me it was the little trivial everyday things that you couldn't do that was the most annoying; like running out of ingredients and not being able to just stroll up to the shops to buy some.

'You get used to the noise and bombs and bullets and you end up not being really concerned about getting killed so much as being sick of having this bland rice with no fish sauce', she said.

Tram's jackpot came when she was eleven. She entered a photo competition for kids in the Sunday paper. She was vaguely interested in photography and decided to take this artsy shot of a green, plastic rubbish bin. She sent the photo in and forgot about it.

Two weeks later a letter arrived in the mail telling her she'd won the competition and the prize was a Toyworld voucher for $500. We couldn't believe it. She shared the bounty with us and we split the voucher three ways. We went from having no money to having $500 to spend on anything we wanted in a toyshop. We spent hours deciding what to buy and it was such a happy day. Tram has since grown up to become a successful photographer.

Tram always looked after Khoa and me as though she was our older sister. By this time Grandma had moved out and Tram had to grow up quickly, helping me cook, clean and do other household chores while Mum was working. I remember her standing on a stool to reach up to the sink just so she could wash the dishes.

At the start of every year St Aloysius gave you a list of textbooks you needed for the semester. Between my brother and I the cost came close to a thousand dollars. Mum simply didn't have the money, and after a while I stopped showing her the list.

'I've got to buy some books, Mum.'

'How much do you need?'

'One hundred, two hundred; whatever you can spare.' I didn't want her to see the list and be burdened by the knowledge that she didn't have enough. It would have devastated her to know that I was missing the required books.

Lucky for me I had my good mate Phil Keenan. Phil was the

only kid in school who knew I didn't have all the books.

'What classes have you got today?' he would ask. When it was English, for example, he would lend me his books for my period and I would return them to him in time for his class. I always had to be thinking about how to plan the day, when to meet up with him, how to make sure the other boys didn't catch on. This concern totally overtook my life; it was all-encompassing and supremely annoying.

Borrowing text books was one thing but then there was the problem with the books that you had to write in. I would sit at my desk and pretend to be writing in Phil's book by hovering my pen above it. The teacher probably thought, *What's wrong with this freak?* To Phil's credit he helped me whenever he could and instinctively knew it was a closely guarded secret.

Sometimes I would get caught out. If Phil was away I would go to English without a book. When the teacher asked where it was, I would lie and say, 'I forgot it'. I was too proud to admit I couldn't afford my own book.

It may seem very trivial, but I would say it was one of the things that hurt the most over my whole school life, when I saw the disappointment in my teachers' eyes when they would give me detention for wearing the wrong thing or for forgetting my text-books. Of course they had to do it—because those were the rules. And they couldn't understand why Anh, who they knew was such a good kid, would every now and then seem to break the rules almost deliberately. I could have gotten off by simply telling them the truth—'My mum doesn't have the money'—but that was never going to happen.

It was round about halfway through Year 10 when I decided enough was enough. I told Mum I hated St Aloysius, it was too far away, taking almost two hours of travel to and from Milsons Point each day. I told her I wanted to attend the local public school. It was a total lie. At the time I was the student council representative (like a class captain), my marks were good and I loved my sport. Most of all I loved my mates. But none of this mattered when weighed up against the hardship my mum was going through and I would've happily given it all up to see her work a little bit less; to have her fall sick less frequently. She saw right through it and flatly refused.

'You're doing well, son. Just a couple more years and you'll have the marks to choose a profession that you'll love and you'll not have to do a crappy job like me.'

My mum is an asthmatic and her breathing is the first sign she's sick. She wheezes loudly and it is a haunting, scary sound that makes my skin crawl. One time Mum was bedridden and Khoa, Tram and I had to bring her food. The next morning she called me into her bedroom and asked me to help her walk to the sewing machine.

'What are you doing, Mum?'

'They're coming to collect this today. If I don't finish we won't get paid, and they won't give me any more work', she wheezed.

'But the doctor said if you don't rest you could seriously harm yourself.'

'I'm all right . . . '

I helped her over to the machine and offered to give her a hand, but it was a buttoner that I was just no good at.

What surprised and even shocked me on this occasion was not Mum's willingness to work but that I, instead of willing her to rest, was secretly hoping she would go on, keep sewing, even at the risk of her becoming seriously ill. The fear of having no money was so merciless and so overwhelming.

It's a horrible feeling—shame mixed with desperation. I once had an acquaintance who was a junkie and he explained to me about his shame of breaking into his own mum and dad's house to steal from them, just so he could get his next fix. I felt the same watching my sick mother sew those garments.

My mum has a genius streak that is not always present at the exact time she is performing the act of genius.

When I was fifteen, we were pretty close to being flat out broke. It was round about this time when a distant cousin, three times removed, arrived from Vietnam with her daughter and went to stay with relatives. It turned out that a number of family issues, secrets and lies that had happened years and years ago came to the surface, and this poor young woman faced being without a place to live in a new, foreign, intimidating country.

'Come live with us', my mother insisted.

I couldn't believe what Mum was offering. Financially we were struggling, desperately struggling, and she'd just offered a young woman and her five-year-old daughter a place to stay.

'They've got no one', she said.

'Are they going to pay rent and stuff?' Khoa piped up.

'If they can, they will. If they can't, what does it matter?' And that was that. We knew not to argue with Mum when it came to giving. The next day the young mother and her daughter moved in with us.

Somehow, though, it didn't seem like we had to do with less at all. It felt like exactly the opposite. Having this woman stay with us made us feel very well off. This is why my mum is a genius. She could've told us a million times that we were lucky to have what we had—three meals a day, clothes to wear, a roof over our heads—and we would never have believed her because we heard these clichés all the time and they didn't make us feel lucky. But allowing someone who had even less than we did to live with us made us feel incredibly fortunate, wealthy even. This woman was so appreciative and grateful, and always made us feel like we were benefactors sent from God to help her through.

Six months after they moved in Mum assisted the woman to find a job and before long she was off, just like that, ready to start her life again. Every Christmas she sent us a card to let us know how she was doing and that was enough for Mum. It was a pattern in our life that I had grown to expect and even to enjoy. Over the years there had probably been a few dozen people, ranging from uncles to single mums to old ladies, come and stay with us, and it is a part of my childhood I wouldn't change. I learned life experiences from a whole range of people, and it was an incredibly rich and varied form of wisdom that these passers-by gifted us with.

I played basketball for a while at school. The best way to describe my teammates was by their shoes: three Reebok Pumps, four Air Jordans, and a Nike Max Lite. My shoes were called 'Kind Lion'— someone at the Chinese factory must have stuffed up the translation. My mother bought them from an Asian grocery store in Bankstown for $15. They featured a lion running across the sides and were made of plastic and vinyl.

The vinyl didn't breathe and the shoes made my feet smell like three-day-old road kill that had been hit while eating parmesan cheese. However, I soon learned that if you played well enough, the other kids would lay off your badly named shoes, and so I decided to practise every day.

We bought a second-hand basketball ring and I bolted it onto the side of the house and shot hoops with Khoa. I'd never put so much practise into a sport, but I had a very good incentive. The school had an endorsement deal with the local sports shop: if any kid reached thirty points in a game, they won a new pair of shoes.

Throughout a whole season there might be only two or three kids who got there. At our level, the whole team together would usually reach only thirty or forty points in total. I was an A's player in the Under 13s, playing with hotshots who were really good. While I was scoring the occasional basket, I was never going to

get anywhere near thirty. So at the start of the Under 14s I deliberately played as bad as possible, skipped training sessions, ate pizza
just before games, shot poorly and played lazy in defence. Within a
couple of weeks, I had successfully been promoted (at least in my
mind) into the Ds.

Whoo-hoo! Let my season begin!

I soon learned that it was even harder to score thirty in the Ds
than the As because the guys around you were freakin' hopeless. It
took me all season to get even close, but my big chance came in the
last game of the season against Barker College. With seven minutes
to go, I was on twenty-four points.

'This guy is everywhere', my Irish coach shouted out to his
bench. 'He deserves a rest. Anh, take a break!' he called to me. I was
shattered. He had no idea about the score I was going for. I sat down
for about thirty seconds then jumped up again.

'Sir, sir, can I go back on for the last five minutes?'

'Nah, we've got the game won. Relax son—you've earned it.'
Luckily, Phil piped up.

'No, sir, you don't understand. Anh's on twenty-four and he only
needs six more to win a pair of High Top Reebok Pumps.'

'Jaysus! Why didn't you tell me earlier you daft eediot! Anh, next
time-out you're on.'

New shoes here I come baby! I leapt on to the court. My teammates
knew exactly what was going on.

'Give Anh the shot!'

I had three minutes to score six points, the entire team conspiring to get me there, and a killer hook-shot that no opposition D's
player could stop. All I needed was for my shoes to hold up.

The entire season I had punished my kings of the jungle, and
they were turning into tired, pissed-off lions that had had a gutful of
my stinky feet running them ragged. I'd played the last three games
with virtually zero grip left on them, so at every break I ran to the
side of the court, poured some lemonade on the ground and then

walked around in the puddle to sticky up my soles. On this fateful day, I'd run out of lemonade.

Nooooooo!

'No worries', said Phil. 'I'll go buy some from the vending machine.' Phil came back quick smart . . . with a can of Diet Coke.

'What? Where's the lemonade?' I asked.

'You're only going to use a bit of it, I thought I could drink the rest; and my mum wants me to stick to Diet Coke.'

Whatever, I thought. *A soft drink is a soft drink.* I poured the Diet Coke onto the ground and gave lion one and lion two a much-needed sip. I handed the can back to Phil, who started guzzling like a thirsty refugee.

'Whoa. Save some for me, Phil. Don't drink it all.'

I rushed back onto the court and in about five seconds I realised something wasn't right. The Diet Coke had absolutely zero effect on my grip. In fact, it seemed to make my shoes glide across the court's surface. I slipped, slid, fell over and played the worst three minutes of my basketball career. My twenty-four points remained just that and I never got those High Top Reebok Pumps with the little orange inflator device. The whistle went at the end of the game and I walked off the court. Everyone was stunned.

'What happened?' says Phil.

'I had no grip whatsoever.'

He looked down at the Diet Coke.

'The stickyness must come from the sugar.'

The next summer Phil decided to swap games and play cricket and asked me to switch as well so we could still hang out. I knew absolutely nothing about cricket, not even the backyard variety. Other kids had a backyard to play in, mine was filled with Grandma's vegies, two ducks and a golden pheasant.

These are photos Grandma brought over to Australia when she arrived years after our boat trip.

Mum and Dad at their wedding ceremony. The local kids made sure they got into the photo. One of them managed to only get his foot in (lower left).

In this photo I am two years old. It's just a few months before our boat trip. (L to r) Dad, Auntie Ten, me, Khoa, Mum.

Mum and Dad at their wedding reception. The family all chipped in so they could enjoy a happy wedding banquet, albeit in a modest restaurant.

A Vietnamese refugee boat being towed, courtesy of the UN. Our boat was crowded much like this one. (UNHCR/ K. Gaugler)

Shortly after we arrived in Australia. The clothes we are wearing were given to us by St Vincent de Paul nuns. The little one in the white dress is my brother Khoa. Back Row (l to r): Uncle Thanh, Auntie Huong, Mum, Dad, Uncle Dai, Uncle Khanh, Uncle Dung. Front row: Khoa, me.

Khoa and me. When the nuns gave us clothes, the only apparel that would fit Khoa were girls' clothes. Hahahahaha.

Khoa (left) eventually turned back into a boy.

Tram's christening outside St Brigid's Church, Marrickville. Uncle Two (far right) is the one with the missing finger and Uncle Eight (second from right) is the one who swallowed the jewellery.

Happy family at Tram's fourth birthday.

At Tram's fifth birthday we are joined by our cousins. (L to r) Me, Dung, Manh, Tram, Grandma, Tri, Khoa.

The Dos executing break dancing moves at a Christmas party. We were encouraged to perform at every family gathering. (L to r) Me, Khoa, Dung and Tri.

Dad being funny at a friend's wedding. He was filling in for the MC who didn't show and made things up as he went along. Watching him as a kid influenced my decision to become a comedian.

I was good looking when I was six.

Mum posing as if she was on the cover of a magazine. Dad used to tell us: 'Your mum's beautiful enough to be a model'. They adored each other.

Khoa and me on the trip to Melbourne with Uncle Six. I am wearing the Balmain Tigers jacket that Uncle Six gave me. Khoa is eating.

Christmas time. The kid in the middle got a transformer robot ... Khoa and I got pictures of Jesus and Mary. Check out Khoa's smartypants fake excitement.

Me and Dad. Those pictures of Jesus and Mary made it to the living room shelves.

Khoa, Dad and me enjoying good times. In the six months after this photo was taken, Dad went into a spiral of decline and eventually left.

Khoa and me as teenagers. Khoa lost a lot of weight after Dad left.

One of the few photos of Tram smiling as a child. She was very self conscious of her teeth.

Tram and me on her wedding day. Big beautiful smile!

Mum, Tram and me. Good times.

'Nah, I've never played before, I don't even have a bat.'

'Doesn't matter. I've got heaps of spare gear I can lend you.'

'Sweet.'

That was all the encouragement I needed. My biggest concern at the beginning of each sports season was whether I had the right equipment or not. I once considered playing tennis but only for as long as it took me to walk into Rebel Sport and see the prices of racquets.

At the time my Kind Lions were in tatters and my basketball singlet was so small it used to ride up my back every time I took a shot, so Phil's offer came like a rescue chopper in the night. Before long we found ourselves in the Es together.

I soon realised that switching to cricket was the biggest mistake I'd ever made. I was totally hopeless at it. I was near the bottom of the batting order and I never got to bowl either, except on one very memorable occasion.

Around the middle of the season we were playing Cranbrook. They had this kid who was just impossible to get out. He was on about sixty runs or so, which was huge for a schoolboy Es team. Our whole squad had tried to bowl him out with no success. The coach thought he might as well chuck me in there.

'Let's give Anh a bowl. Where's Anh?'

I was somewhere in the outfield, probably watching the bees hop from daisy to daisy.

'Anh, come in for a bowl?' It was half a command, half a question; the coach half hoping I would say no.

'C'mon, have a go', Phil called out.

'I don't want to', I replied.

'This guy's smashing everyone, so it doesn't matter. You can't stuff up', Phil said.

It turned out I could. I couldn't get the ball to stay on the pitch and bowled a whole bunch of wides. The kid batting was getting frustrated because the balls were nowhere near close enough for him to hit. I turned to Phil as if to say, 'I told you so'. It was so embarrass-ing that even the parents watching started chipping in. Some old guy from the sidelines yelled out 'just try and get it to go straight', and I could hear the mothers laughing at me.

I grabbed the ball and bowled another shocking delivery. The kid was so frustrated he ran four feet wide of the wicket and took a wild swing at the ball, which flew straight up into the air to be caught by my wicket keeper. Out!

WHOO-HOO!!!

All my teammates ran over and mobbed me, we all knew it was a complete fluke, but it didn't matter. I handed the ball back to my coach, thinking it was all over and had ended sweetly.

'Ah, no, Anh. Because of all the wides, you've got four more balls.'

Oh man, I thought to myself.

The next kid walked up to the crease. His coach had seen what had happened and he told this kid, 'Don't try and hit it if it's nowhere near you. Just leave it.'

I came steaming in from my 'long run' and lobbed the ball in the new batsman's direction . . . it was so wide it landed on the very edge of the pitch where the concrete joined the longer grass of the field. Hitting that uneven line made it bounce back in and the poor kid watched it roll slowly behind him and dribble into the stumps. He hadn't even touched the ball and I had got him out.

WHOO-BLOODY-HOO!!!!

I was mobbed again.

'Mate, you're on a hat-trick', Phil ran over to tell me.

'What's that again?' I asked. I had heard the term before but I didn't really know what it meant. Phil explained that if I got the next batsman out on his first ball, that would make three wickets in three balls—a hat-trick. Our coach was beaming and he said, 'In all my years at this school, I have never seen anyone do it.'

Now even I was excited.

Alas, the new batsman was onto me and he whacked my next three balls all over the shop. So much for the hat-trick. But at the end of the year my stats showed me bowling one over, taking two wickets and conceding less than twenty runs, so I had the best bowling average in the whole school. I never played cricket again, but the experience was such a valuable lesson in my life. Since then, whenever I've had to go into battle as the underdog, I know in my heart that an extraordinary result is a very possible outcome.

I hated homework. I hated it most when it took time away from helping Mum out with the sewing. It didn't take me long to find a solution.

The train trip from school to home took around fifty minutes, so I'd hop on the train at the end of each day, find a corner seat and rip through my homework as fast as possible. Many teachers commented over the years how bad my handwriting was, but what they didn't know was that I was mostly writing on the rattling 3.35 p.m. from Milson's Point to Yagoona. Most days I finished all my homework before Wiley Park Station and I'd sit there and stare dreamily out the window, satisfied that I was completely done.

One semester, I had a couple of free periods after lunch on Thursdays, which meant I could go home at 1 p.m. These were great days because I got to go home early and the train was always empty. I could choose any seat I wanted, even flip three over and have six seats to myself, like a private sleeper compartment.

One afternoon I was alone in the carriage. The train stopped at Redfern and a group of three guys, about sixteen or seventeen years old, wearing baseball caps, baggy pants and the rest, got on. They came over and one of them sat next to me, the other two opposite.

'Can I borrow a dollar?' the skinniest one of them said. I didn't think anything of it. I'd never been mugged before and I really thought this guy just wanted to borrow a buck. Maybe he'd return it next time I saw him, maybe not?

'I don't have any money', I said with a straight face.

'I don't believe you, show me your wallet.'

This is when I tweaked I was being rolled. My mind spun as I mentally scoured my wallet to see if I really didn't have any money. Usually my wallet was completely empty, but every now and then I carried more money than any kid in the whole school. Other kid's parents wrote cheques for their school fees that were mailed in like clockwork, but we were a bit different. Mum had never owned a chequebook, so every now and then she would look in her little green money sock and see whether she'd scraped together enough money to pay part of the two years' worth of fees we owed. I panicked when I remembered that very morning Mum had handed me a bulging envelope.

Jesus, Mary and Michael Jackson. Of all the days . . . have I given the money to the bursar or is it still in my wallet? I wasn't sure. I thought to myself, *I need to buy some time here to think.*

One of the guys, a huge chubby bloke who looked like his head had been squeezed into too small a face and his cheeks were busting to get out, was wearing an LA Lakers' cap.

'You like the Lakers too?' I asked.

'Yeah', he smiled back.

'Shut up, will ya?' the skinny guy said to chubby, then turned to me. 'Give us your wallet', he demanded, this time more menacingly.

My mind was in total panic mode now. I *thought* I'd handed the envelope over to Mrs Watkins that morning, but the threat of a beating or worse made me uncertain. *Geez, I wish we weren't on a train 'cos I reckon I can outrun these guys. Maybe fight the pricks. I might not win, but I'd win some time and someone might come and help me.*

I slowly reached my hand in my pocket and pulled out my wallet. As the guy opened it up, I was looking just as closely as he was to see what was in there.

Ahhh. Relief. No crumpled envelope full of tens and twenties or the occasional fiver that was bent at the edges—like notes get when they have been sitting in a Vietnamese woman's sock for six months.

'Shit, aye. You really got nothin'.' Then the skinny guy pulled out my school train pass, the only thing that was worth anything and chucked me back my wallet.

'Don't take his train pass, dickhead', the chubby guy piped up. 'You don't look like a . . .' he peered over the shoulder of his skinny mate and tried to read my name '. . . Anne Doo . . . Arhh Doh . . . you got a funny name, aye?'

The skinny guy flicked the train pass back at me and the three of them took off.

Thank you, thank you, thank you, Mum and Dad for giving me one of the hardest names to pronounce. This was one of the few times in my life where it turned into an advantage.

I was incredibly relieved as it would have taken forever to apply for a new train pass and Mum would've had to have forked out a few hundred dollars for three months worth of Yagoona to Milson's Point, five days a week. I sat as still as I could and decided to get off the train at the next stop to catch another one, just in case skinny guy changed his mind and thought he could pass himself off as a kid called Anne Doo.

The next stop was Strathfield and we were only a few minutes away when I heard a huge commotion—swearing, shouting and the familiar crunching of punches landing into a face. I looked up and there were the three guys laying into another guy who was sitting alone. After hearing about all my dad's heroics, I had always imagined that in a situation like that I would not hesitate to jump in and do the right thing. Instead I just sat there and watched, frozen in fear as the chubby baby-faced giant pounded his ham-like fist into the back of the guy's head, flinging blood and saliva onto the train window.

Strathfield arrived like an oasis. The doors of the train opened and the three guys got out and ran off, carrying with them the loot, a pair of Reebok Pumps. Lucky for me, a couple of weeks earlier Phil had purchased that can of Diet Coke, otherwise I would've been the kid bashed for his shoes.

What does a fourteen-year-old kid do when he wants to make money? A paper run.

'I'm going to help you out, Mum. I got a job!'

'Doing what?'

'Delivering pamphlets.'

'What about homework?'

'I'll fit it in.'

'Do it if you really want to. But if you're doing it for money, then don't.'

I told her I really wanted to. As always, she saw right through me.

'No, I don't want you to do it.'

I persisted, telling her it was part of my growing up, blah blah blah, until eventually, she agreed to let me try.

I had asked the woman at the pamphlet company to deliver the largest amount possible. It was to arrive on the Monday and had to be put in the letterboxes by the Wednesday. On Monday morning an enormous stack of boxes rocked up on our doorstep, and all day at school I was looking forward to coming home and starting my new job. The thought of earning cash was such a thrill.

By the time I got back from school a colossal afternoon storm broke open the sky and it bucketed down. I figured, *No problem, I'll start tomorrow.* Tuesday afternoon and I was raring to go. I emptied my schoolbag of books and chocked it full of pamphlets. It weighed about forty kilograms. It wasn't even a proper backpack with padding or support, just a sports bag design. I slung the straps over my shoulders and it was lumpy and unbalanced.

Four hours and around ten kilometres of walking later, I had delivered only about a quarter of the pamphlets. On Wednesday night I needed to complete the whole lot so I was off again, this time with Khoa on the other side of the road. We would do a loop around a block, covering both sides. We promised each other we would keep going till we finished.

Ten p.m. that night we slumped into bed absolutely exhausted. We still had about a third to go.

'Mum, there's too many.'

'That's all right, we'll finish it tomorrow. It'll be a day late but once you start a job you've got to finish it. I'll help you.'

The next night Khoa, Mum, Tram and me hit the foothpath, working like machines, this time with the car assisting us. (Mum locked the pamphlets in the boot so we didn't have to walk back home to get more.) What seemed like an eternity later we finally finished. It was way past Tram's bedtime and I realised that this job was just too much work—I'd never intended for my whole family to have to labour with me; the idea was for Mum to work less, not to have her trek around after dark for hours.

Mum put the others to bed and came over to me, sitting at a table madly trying to squeeze in my homework. She put her hand on my shoulder and I stopped writing and looked up into a mother's loving face.

'Thank you, Anh, but this is too much. You keep doing well at school, and I will take care of the money.'

It turned out Mum was better at taking care of the money than me. Despite all our effort, the pamphlets were delivered late and the woman didn't even pay us.

I was feeling pretty dejected after my first attempt at being an employee but I still wanted to somehow make money and help out Mum. The solution came in the form of a large male Siamese fighting fish.

My dad had bought a fish tank at auction many, many years ago, and the previous Christmas Uncle Dung had bought Khoa and me a few fish to stick in it. We had a few guppies and swordtails, but what I really wanted was a couple of Siamese fighting fish. When we were kids we would often visit a pet shop for a look, and Dad was the self-proclaimed expert on these fish. Within a few seconds of spotting a male, he could tell you whether it would win or lose in a fight against another male.

'The long colourful fins are for show and get ripped up easy, causing body injuries. What you're after is the ugliest one with short stumpy fins and a fat body.' Dad would point to a blocky little nugget of a fighter at the front of the tank.

'See that one? Not much to look at, but it will beat all these other ones easy. That one there—he is the fish-world's Mike Tyson.'

His theories sounded plausible enough, but he could've been making the whole thing up. One day at the aquarium we decided to test out his ideas. My brother looked for the most beautiful long-finned male, and I picked the short stumpy Mike Tyson one. We planned to let them loose on each other. We figured we wouldn't get them to fight to the death or anything like that; after all they were $9.95 each. But maybe they could fight just till you could see who was winning, then we could send in a pack of goldfish to drag them apart and say, 'Leave it out you two. It ain't worf it.'

As an adult, I have to say I am appalled at the thought of getting animals to fight, but we were young teenage boys back then. We took the beautiful one and the Tyson one home and plopped them into the tank, separated by a glass divider screen so that we could feed and fatten them up—prepare them like heavyweight contenders before the main event. In our young minds they were staring at each other like two prizefighters before a weigh in. I imagined mine was saying in fish-talk to psyche out the other one:

'What are *you* lookin at, fin boy?'

The other replied: 'Float like a butterfly-fish, sting like an anemone.'

We took it pretty seriously. About a week later our fish were plump, glistening with muscles and raring to go. Khoa was betting that his beautiful long-finned one was going to win; it was much bigger than mine. But I *knew* mine was going to win. I had the nuggety one.

We lifted the tank divider screen with anticipation . . .

Wham!

Straight away, Fin Boy chased mine into the corner, and then . . . totally lost all interest.

Huh? we thought. *That's it?*

'Fight! Fight! Fight! Fight!' we chanted.

Nothing. They just swam around with the other fish and didn't even notice each other at all. We were absolutely shattered. What a disappointment.

Khoa was especially pissed. 'Dad's full of it, man. That guy's probably never even seen a fish-fight. He's full of crap. There's more crap coming out of him than currently trailing behind Fin Boy.'

Khoa and I grew up never really knowing what to believe and what not to believe about Dad. So often we had heard him tell us about something he had done and not really believed it, or thought that he was exaggerating. Later we'd overhear others talking, confirming his truth. He was such a larger-than-life character who lived in the exaggerated circumstances of a war. We eventually learned not to doubt the length and breadth of his adventures or, at times, his stupidity.

'Should we separate them again?' my brother asked. 'Just in case they fight later?'

'Nah, they're not even taking any notice of each other.'

So we left them there and went and played with our footy cards.

The next morning Khoa and I woke up to find Fin Boy and Mr Tyson embraced in an intense lock of fins and scales. But rather than looking aggressive and violent, it seemed more . . . beautiful and affectionate. They were engaged in a rolling dance, spiralling down to the bottom of the tank and then rising again, like a yoyo with red fins. It turned out they weren't fighting at all, they were breeding.

Mr Tyson was a Mrs Tyson, and our two Siamese fighting fish were making babies. When they were staring each other out, it wasn't the fighting talk like I'd imagined. Fin Boy was saying, 'Hey, gorgeous, how you doin'?'

Before long there were babies everywhere. We raised the young fry up until they were shop size then took them down to our local aquarium. Three dollars per fish! *Whoo-hoo!!!*

We made sixty bucks. I quickly did the maths and discovered that there were other breeds that had several hundred babies at a time. So three bucks times say, four hundred babies—that's one thousand two hundred big ones! Get a bunch of tanks happening and you could have twelve hundred coming in every month. And the best part of it was the fish did all the work for you.

I was starting to think just like my dad—fast, big and over the top. Pretty soon we had about twenty fish tanks. We didn't have enough money to buy the tanks so I built a heap of them myself. Any glass that was left out on the road I brought home. If someone left out an old window to be taken away, I'd chuck it into the back of the car, set to it with a glass-cutter and some silicon, and turn it into a tank. Then came my piece de resistance: an enormous display aquarium, nearly two metres wide. It carried almost a thousand litres of water and was decked out with heaters, lights, filters, rocks, caves and plants. It was like Disneyland for fish, with everything a fish could ever desire. They didn't care if it was made from second-hand freebies from the local aquarium club; to them it was a luxurious honeymoon suite, designed and tailor-made to put anything with fins in the mood for loving. And it accommodated about a hundred of my biggest and best-breeding adult specimens, who were going at it like Catholic Spaniards on their wedding night.

Everything was going well, until about 2 a.m. one fateful night when I was woken by an enormous *Boom!* that sounded like New Year's Eve fireworks. Except fireworks don't have just one boom followed by an even louder scream from my mum.

Khoa and I jumped out of bed and sprinted into the lounge room. The giant fish tank had split in the corner. Fishworld had opened up because I hadn't put enough silicon on the joins. We watched, stunned, as a thousand litres of water poured onto the carpet, fish flopping everywhere.

Mum and Tram raced around the kitchen and found every single pot, pan, cup and bowl they could. Soon every container was filled with bewildered looking fish, who stared at me like angry hotel guests who've been sent outside when a fire alarm goes off in the middle of the night.

Suddenly there was a pungent burning smell and I could hear a buzzing noise. I looked into the corner and saw the water lapping up against two four-way power boards stacked high with cords. *Fizz, fizz, crackle.*

'Oh my god, electricity! Everyone get out!' Mum screamed. She was worried about her children; I was worried about my fish.

'I'll turn it off', I shouted. Everyone else screamed, 'No'.

I reached my hand in and flicked the switch. An almighty shock tore up my arm and sent me flying backwards, landing on two Chinese takeaway containers, and sending a family of bristlenose catfish flying against the wall. Mum ran towards me but Khoa held her back.

'Mum, stop! Don't touch him.'

Luckily, I was all right. All the lights on the left side of the house went out as the safety switch kicked into gear. I got up, still feeling that strange, jolting energy pulsing through me.

'No worries, the electricity's off.'

Then we packed all the fish into containers. The floor was covered in water. We stayed up for a few hours mopping it all up, and finally went back to sleep. The carpet stunk of aquarium water for over a year, and for all that time the air remained damp and foul. But I am proud to say that not a single fish died that night. My mother was relieved that not a single child died that night either.

Every now and then Mum likes to bring up the electric shock story.

'Why does Anh drink too much beer?'

'He got the shock when he was fourteen.'

'Why did Anh come second on *Dancing with the Stars*?'

'That time he got shocked . . . makes him jerk around like a frog when he dances.'

'Is that shock why Anh is so good at comedy as well?'

'Oh no, that's 'cos he takes after his mum.'

One of the best things about St Aloysius was its focus on developing the 'well rounded' young man. So rather than just offering academics and sport, it encouraged a lot of co-curricular activities as well; chess, for example.

I represented the school at chess for exactly one game. The Year 9 chess team was missing a few guys, even the reserves were away at a camp, and we would've forfeited a loss if no one could attend the event. Terry, Phil and Lloydy were playing and, although I'd never played before, they said they'd teach me at lunchtime. There are quite a few games you can learn in a school lunchtime. Noughts and crosses, snakes and ladders, bullrush—you can learn all these in about ten minutes. Chess, however, takes a bit longer. In the afternoon the school team from Trinity arrived and, rook me dead, I still didn't know my knight from my pawn.

In the chess comp the players would be ranked one to four—one being the best player and four the worst. We would then play the other school's corresponding one to four players. Of course I should've been number four. But I came up with a plan.

'Why don't I be number one?' I said to the boys. 'That way I can cop a loss to their number one player and our number one player would play their two and have a better chance. Our number two would play their number three, and so on.' I figured I was going to lose anyway, and this strategy would give the other three boys a bigger chance of winning because they were effectively playing against someone ranked lower than them.

Brilliant!

Trinity's chess team rocked up and I was introduced to this lanky Indian kid with a huge gap between his two front teeth. Having only been in a competitive situation on the footy field before, I tried to stare him out like you do when you line up against your opponents in football. He clearly didn't quite understand why I was giving him the hairy eyeball, and his puzzled look was so disarming I gave up my intimidation tactic. We sat down, flipped a coin and he made a move. He then switched on a little timer clock to make sure I didn't take more than sixty seconds to decide my move. I looked at the board and figured I'd take as long as possible—I stroked my chin, furrowed my brow, tried to look like I was thinking of a king-hit manoeuvre. I picked up a piece and plonked it down on a square.

He stared at it in dismay.

Yeah, take that buddy! I think to myself. *I've got the guy rattled already.*

'You can't do that', he said.

'Why not?'

'Because it's against the rules.'

'I was just kidding, just seeing if you know how to play', I said, taking my horsey piece back and moving it elsewhere.

'You can't move it now. Once you take your hand off a piece it has to stay there.'

Well what the hell do you want me to do, Einstein? I couldn't leave it there, I couldn't move it to another spot—what was I supposed to do, make it float in mid air or something?

'Okay, you can leave it there', he said. We started trading moves and I'm thinking, *What a condescending smarty-pants. Now I'm going to really kick his arse. I'm going to take this guy apart piece by smarty-pants piece. I'm going to . . .*

'Checkmate.'

What? In eleven moves? Is that some sort of record?

Terry had told me at lunchtime that when they say 'checkmate' it meant they'd beaten you—game over.

My opponent grinned, then sighed: 'Have you ever played chess before?'

'Of course I have. Heaps. I just have good days and not-so-good days, and you are lucky 'cos today is probably one of my less good days.'

'You've never played before, have you?'

'Nuh.'

'My mum's not picking me up till five o'clock. Wanna play again?'

'All right.'

The second time he beat me in nine moves.

His long, scrawny fingers put one of my pieces back on the board and he said, 'If you did this, that would've stopped me from being able to beat you, that's why I said check. It means I am in a position to win so you have to defend yourself.'

'Right. And that piece can move anywhere 'cos it's the queen?'

'Correct. And that horsey piece is actually called a knight.'

Over the next hour and a half this guy taught me how to play chess. He even showed me a couple of tricks you can use against novice players that hand you the win very quickly.

Five o'clock arrived and I bid farewell to my former chess opponent and now mentor. I rushed out of the room and eagerly asked the others how they went—did I take a bullet for the team for a worthy win?

'Terry?'

'Lost.'

'Phil?'

'Lost.'

'Lloydy?'

'Lost.'

We realised that we could've forfeited, kicked a footy around for two hours, and achieved exactly the same result.

My high school also had a lot of volunteer programs with different charity groups and strongly encouraged students to lend a hand as a way of developing empathy and compassion for those less fortunate. The program wasn't compulsory but my mother was absolutely emphatic about me participating in it.

'You have to do it. This is just as important as getting good marks.' Charity work touched a chord with her.

At fifteen I spent a few weeks as a volunteer at a homeless shelter. There was an old man, about sixty, who was withdrawing from drugs. One day he walked past me to get to the bathroom. He didn't make it. Suddenly he threw up everywhere. The vomit came out of his mouth, his nose and his eyes. *Out of his eyes for god's sake!* This browny liquid just oozed out of him and a strange odour of rotten fish mixed with diarrhoea filled the air. I had to try my best not to vomit myself. In that instant, which I have never forgotten, I vowed never to touch drugs. So, even later on in my comedy years, when temptation started popping up everywhere, I may have played up till all hours, but I never touched drugs.

I'm pleased to say I never once suffered any racism at school from my mates or fellow students. My only experience of something odd in relation to my nationality came from one of my teachers—a history teacher.

I first sensed something strange in the way he would use particular words that even back then weren't a hundred per cent okay in the classroom. The first lesson we had with him he held up a dark folder and described its colour as 'boong black', and the kids laughed. At the time I knew boong was a derogatory term for Aborigines but I didn't think too much of it. Maybe he was just trying to get in with us by being politically incorrect to get a laugh, so I let it go. Then in the second lesson we were introduced to the 1850s gold rush in rural Australia, and he gave the class an unusual assignment. We had to make posters from the gold rush period but not just any old posters. He wanted us to create modern-day versions of the anti-Asian posters that the settlers made during the time following the arrival of Chinese prospectors in the goldfields. Basically, the class were told they were to spend an entire Year 9 history period drawing up posters that made fun of Asians.

What the hell is the point of this? I thought to myself. *What are we learning here?* He showed us pictures of the posters made back in the 1850s with the exaggerated Asian man's face with buck teeth, slanty eyes and racists slogans: 'The Yellow Peril will steal your livelihood and rape your women', etc., etc. Was I supposed to join in or sit on a stool and pose, like it was a 'life drawing' class?

So everyone started working on their posters, and the teacher encouraged us with examples of negative behaviour by Asians through-out history. Then towards the end of the period he asked if anyone wanted to come up the front and show everyone else their poster. So fourteen-year-old boys began getting up in front of the class and were not just allowed, but were encouraged, to say racists things.

I was the only Asian student in the class and I felt terrible. I was especially angry at him for the insidious way he was getting my mates, whom I knew weren't racist at all, to say things they would never say to me. It wasn't enough that this guy hated Asians and Aborigines, he was trying to convert the class as well.

It was such a strange situation. I had a whole year of this subject ahead of me and I knew the guy had a problem with the way I looked, my race—something I couldn't change or do anything about. It never occurred to me to tell another teacher about him, so I did the only thing I knew to do with a teacher: I tried to win his approval. And I think I did. Weirdly, by the end of the year I think the guy quite liked me.

I look back on it now and I believe if I had my time again I would do things differently. A part of me is quite ashamed of my cowardice at the time, for trying to make this guy like me. But mostly I am understanding of a kid who was merely trying to not stand out.

What I've found with racism in Australia is that there are isolated and one-off incidents, but wider Australia is appalled by it. The reaction against a racist act is always quick and severe. The Cronulla riots in 2005 are a good example. A few incidents had occurred to set off a group of young men who got drunk, draped the Australian flag on their shoulders and began bashing anyone of Middle Eastern appearance. When the rest of Australia saw this, the wave of disgust was enormous and all-encompassing. I found the same thing to be true on a much smaller scale, like on the football field.

I only ever experienced racism on the field a handful of times, and every time someone made me feel like an outsider, my team-mates very quickly let me know I was very much on the inside. When I was playing for my beloved Merrylands Rams, an opposition player called out, 'I'm going to smash the gook'. Immediately my mates rallied around me.

'Number four's just called Anh a gook!'

The message went around and for the rest of the game my Aussie teammates belted the living daylights out of this guy every time he got the ball.

In my final year, a man from the army came to our school and told us about the army reserves. He said a whole bunch of stuff that I don't really remember, trying to get us to join. He was a pretty boring guy, and the only time I laughed was when Phil said to me, 'Man, imagine getting stuck in a foxhole with this guy? You'd listen to that voice drone on for maybe one or two days at the most, and then you'd have to shoot him yourself.'

The monotone army guy then said something that suddenly made him very interesting.

'You get paid $15 000 a year.'

Fifteen grand a year!

'For a few weeks of training and a commitment to the Australian armed forces, we'll pay you $15 000 a year.'

An extra 15K a year would just about double what Mum was bringing home. All of a sudden this big doofus talking to us didn't seem so bad. *Geez, he isn't that boring after all, compared to Mr Finch he's a natural orator.* (Mr Finch was our Religion teacher who dribbled a bit when he talked, but didn't realise it until his saliva was halfway out, and then he sucked it back into his mouth without breaking his sentence.)

I signed up for an army scholarship as soon as the talk was over. They scheduled an interview for me for the following weekend. For the rest of the afternoon I daydreamed through all my classes as I entertained the thought of joining the army. I got incredibly excited about it. All these years of listening to my dad and uncles talking about the amazingly brave things they did during the war, and here was my chance to out-do them—even though there was no war going on at the time, or at least none that Australia was involved in. *Doesn't matter, I'll become one of those special ops guys that go into war zones and saves the president with only his bare hands.* The movie *Navy Seals* had just come out with Charlie Sheen in the lead role, and I reckoned I would look pretty good in black cargo pants too. The army guy had mentioned free clothes.

I ran home that afternoon and told Mum all about it, how I was going to double our income, and how we were going to be sweet, and how she might as well go out to Kmart right now and buy herself a new dress!

'You're not joining the army', she said.

'*What?* Didn't you hear me? *Fifteen thousand dollars!*'

'No.'

Mum was adamant. I was adamant too. I decided to go ahead with it and forged her signature on all the forms and enrolled. I figured I'd sort it out later, maybe after they paid me and I showed her the cash; that would bring her around. I'd get her those new shoes she'd been checking out in the latest Target catalogue. I would walk right in through the front door and wave those red loafers around. Once she got a whiff of that genuine imitation leather she'd change her mind and congratulate me for disobeying her.

The enrolment was quite a long process. They screened you for a whole bunch of stuff, from academic marks to IQ to your involvement in sport and athletics, and I passed all of it. Then came the interview.

I got along with the interviewer really well. We were talking about all the sports I played—rugby and basketball and a whole bunch of other things—and I was on a roll. Finally the interviewer asked me if I had any health issues.

'No, well, not unless you count asthma.'

'You have asthma?'

'Yeah, why?' I said, slightly concerned by his tone of voice.

'I'm sorry, Anh, we can't take you if you have asthma.'

Shit, quick . . . think of a way out: 'Did I say I have asthma? I meant I'm from Alaska.' *No, that won't work.* I racked my brain for a back pedal but found nothing.

'Why don't you take people who have asthma?'

'Because in a situation involving gas masks, you would be unable to use your puffer and you'd put yourself and your unit at risk of harm.'

You're kidding? My Uncle Thanh crawled through the Vietnam jungle with one lung, and you're going to disqualify me for the occasional use of Ventolin?

'Thank you, sir. Thanks for your time', I muttered.

I caught the train back home to Yagoona, conceding defeat. Mum was there when I walked in.

'You didn't get in, did you?'

'Get into what? I don't know what you're talking about.' I really didn't know how the hell she found out.

'Khoa told me all about it. He asked me if he can have your fish.'

'Nah, I didn't get in.'

She comes over and pats me on the back of the head.

'War's taken too many men away from me.'

As the Year 12 exams loomed it was time to pick a course to study after school, and I really had no idea what I wanted to be. I was certain of one thing, though, it had to pay lots of money. One of my teachers somehow worked out my personal circumstances and made a suggestion.

'Anh, you should apply for special consideration. What you're going through at the moment is pretty intense.' In the previous couple of years he'd noticed that my home address had changed six times, our school fees were behind by four or five semesters, and I was falling asleep in class after staying up late helping Mum sew garments.

'Why don't you apply? If you do, you'll get extra marks to get into university and do a degree.'

'No thanks, sir. I'm okay.'

And that was the end of that. I wasn't interested.

I was actually furious at him. I realised that maybe some of the teachers knew of my situation, and I was paranoid that it would get out. 'Anh is poor.' 'Poor Anh, his mum doesn't have any money.' 'Don't you feel so sorry for the poor refugee?' I cringed as I imagined them talking about me. I hated being on the receiving end of sympathy. I remember all through school being determined to prove that I could survive without any outside help.

As a kid there was a period when one particular landlord loved turning up to collect the late rent himself. Many times Mum was at work and I just got sick of telling this guy we'd pay him soon, knowing full well that we weren't going to be able to. So Khoa, Tram and I would hide whenever he showed up and pretended there was no one home. After a while he figured out that there were people inside so he'd walk around the house and look into the windows to try and catch us. It was all strangely terrifying—we knew this guy was just after rent, but the act of hiding from someone in and of itself has the power to put you in a state of fear.

I remember on more than one occasion saying to myself, *I'm so sick of this. As soon as I'm old enough I'm going to earn loads of money and buy Mum the biggest freakin' house in the suburb and we'll all live there together and it will be our house and the whole world can go and get stuffed.*

There seems to be a lie perpetuated at schools, where you are told you have two options if you want to make loads of money: become a doctor, or become a lawyer. No one talks about the rich real-estate investor, the wealthy builder or even the well-to-do plumber. Many a time a plumber has turned up to my house, spent thirty minutes unclogging a drain, and handed over a bill for $300 without batting an eyelid. Not a bad hourly rate. But at the end of school, the money choice was doctor or lawyer.

I've always hated going to the doctor, especially the ones who have a lot of Asian clients. The waiting room always smells like menthol. Every time an Asian person gets sick, they first try the cure-all Tiger Balm. Got a headache? Tiger Balm on the forehead. Got a sore wisdom tooth? Tiger balm on the jaw. Got Haemorrhoids? . . . It's a bit like the dad in the film *My Big Fat Greek Wedding*, who sprays Windex on every ailment. Most people watched that film and laughed at the dad, but my mum watched it and then went out and bought a bottle of Windex for her sore elbow.

I really had one option: become a lawyer. I enrolled in law at the University of Technology in Sydney, and on the very first day I walked in and thought to myself, *This sucks*. There was only one good thing about uni as far as I was concerned.

• Eight •

It was the very first class, on the very first morning of university. We were a bunch of kids just out of high school, all of us nervous and excited and dressed really badly because for many of us it was the first time we had chosen what to wear rather than just slapping on a uniform. I looked around the classroom and caught sight of a tallish blonde girl.

Wow, she's pretty, I thought to myself.

Then the girl turned my way and I quickly looked down at my watch, pretending to be fascinated with the time, taking way too long to see that it was 10.05 a.m. and fifteen seconds . . . sixteen seconds . . . seventeen seconds. I had just finished six years at an all-boys school and my how-to-be-super-smooth-around-girls skills were a little bit rusty. In fact they were non-existent.

Once I had cleverly distracted her by exploring every nook and cranny of my Casio (and totally convinced myself that she must be facing away by now) I turned to sneak another look. She was chatting to a girl, and then she turned in my direction again and smiled. I don't really believe in love at first sight, but if it does exist then I had just been made a victim. I was smitten.

This girl's smile lit up the room. She seemed to emanate a warmth which captivated me. That day, at 10.06 a.m. and eleven seconds precisely, was when time stood still for Anh Do.

Over the next few months I started forming friendships with my classmates and one of my friends was the light-up-the-room-with-a-smile Suzie. After about six months, Suzie and I had become best friends, and she would ring me up after classes and we would talk for three or four hours. I used to heavily favour my left ear for phone conversations, but thanks to Suzie my ears became ambidextrous. After a couple of hours on the left side, my ear was so sore, I learned to switch over to my right ear and listened just as well.

I thought, *Four hours on the phone! Come on, she must like me a little bit.* So I plucked up the courage and one day told her how I felt.

'Suzie ... you know how, umm ... you and me and ... we evidently *[Evidently? Who says 'evidently'? Since when is evidently a word in the 'Smooth Dude Dictionary? I don't even really know what the word means!]* ... umm ... will you want to go date with me?'

In my nervousness, I'd turned into a Vietnamee English student struggling to talk all proper. Suzie gave me a long hug, I smelled her perfume and my heart sang. I was thinking to myself, *This Vietnamese guy going to on a date!*

'I really like you, Anh', she said. 'But kind of more like a friend.'

My heart sank. I somehow managed to mumble, 'No worries, of course, I kind of see you like a friend too, I just thought, you know ... ahh, is that my train I hear?'

My train? We were at Broadway, about a kilometre from Central Station. I hobbled off in a rush, trying to go as fast as I could without running, like an Olympic walker about to get disqualified.

I look back on it now, and if I'm honest there were quite a few reasons why she wouldn't have been interested in me. But I'll list the three that stand out: Most days I wore a flannelette shirt, Target trackie dacks, and sported a gloriously bad mullet. Who was I kidding? I looked like a Vietnamese Billy Ray Cyrus.

My instincts kept telling me that law wasn't for me. The ultra-competitive nature of the course was especially disheartening, and seemed to be missing the point of championing right over wrong. For example, there were times when we got assignments that required us to read say, twenty pages of volume six of the *Law Journal*. The library would have one copy in the reference section, so everyone would have to photocopy the twenty pages and put the book back. I'd go down to the library and find nothing but a big gap between volumes five and seven. Volume six would be missing. This happened again and again and again, and I just couldn't wrap my head around it. Then a librarian mate told me there were one or two selfish students who would photocopy the required pages for themselves and then hide the volume somewhere obscure, like between the books on the mating habits of grasshoppers and those on the buttock tattoos of Male Eastern Samoans. Good luck to the rest of us finding it.

I'd often sit in lectures and fantasise what I would do if I ever caught one of these lowlifes; with one punch I'd make their number six tooth go missing, leaving a big gap between teeth five and seven. I'd then wrap tooth six in some grass, hop over and wedge it between the buttock tattoos of a large male Eastern Samoan. Good luck to them finding it.

Law was perfect for some but not for me, I guess, so I enrolled in a visual arts course at Meadowbank TAFE. And I loved it.

People often asked me why I studied law and art at the same time. 'Why not?' was my answer. If there was a rule saying you couldn't study full time at TAFE and uni simultaneously, I didn't know about it. I've always found that if you apply yourself at the right time with the right intensity, you can accomplish just about anything. So many times in my life I think my naivety about what you supposedly *could* and *couldn't* do helped me make big leaps that others might think were over the top.

Deep down inside I knew I didn't want to be a lawyer, but I was keen to finish the degree because of its value in getting me a job, any sort of job. I soon figured out that you could do the degree without actually being there for most of it. In lectures I'd look around and see that everyone was just phased out, daydreaming. *They may as well not be here at all*, I thought. *Well, I may as well not be here as well.* So I just attended the key lectures—namely, those where they tell you what's going to be in the exam—and then nailed those topics at home in half the time it took a rambling professor to get through his often irrelevant presentation on chapter 47, subsection 12, on the importance of understanding the use of semi-colons in contract law.

Art was the opposite story—I loved being there. It resonated with me that the whole point about art is not to get the diploma, but to *learn the craft*.

So that's how I got through my university years, skipping law classes to be at art classes. Who could blame me? How would you choose to spend six hours: studying the validity of clause 61, or sketching gorgeous nude women. No contest. Not even close.

On the other hand, during this time I dated a number of art girls, but my heart belonged to a law girl. Suzie was no ordinary law girl, anyway. She was a creative spirit, always painting, taking photos and writing beautiful little poems. She'd fallen into law the same way I had—she'd achieved high marks at school so people told her that law was what you did. Suzie was pretty ambivalent about the whole thing too, so while she looked like the perfect student compared to me, she did her fair share of cutting classes, which I always encouraged.

Sometimes I'd sneak into the back of a lecture hall and there she'd be, eyes half closed, head hanging three inches off the desk, almost asleep, and I'd whisper in her ear: 'You want to go and have a coconut ice-cream?'

Wham! We were out of there.

One day at uni everyone was lined up in the corridor waiting to go into class. I was standing there, brooding over whether I should just ditch law altogether, when all of a sudden I caught a glimpse of Suzie walking in from the sunshine with a pink freesia in her hair and a fistful of daffodils for me.

'I picked them for you on the way to the train station.' And there was that amazing smile again.

How many girls nick flowers out of other people's front yards to give to their male friends? None that I've met. If uni was one big, dismal, grey cloudy day, Suzie was the patch of sunlight that breaks through and takes you completely by surprise.

I liked Suzie; I liked her a lot. It felt like I liked her more than what should rightly be described by the word 'like', more like that other L-word. But every time I thought I had a shot, she'd tell me we were 'just friends'.

My grandma knew how to read palms and had taught me a few things when I was a kid. She used to look at the lines on my little hand and explain to me why I was cheerful but impatient, and had horsey teeth. I tried to read Suzie's palm at university one day.

'This looks very interesting. It seems like a man will soon come into your life, he will be stocky, dark and have big teeth . . .'

'Oh my god, I must get some pepper spray!' What a smart aleck.

'Sorry Anh, I've just started seeing someone.'

Damn! Missed the window again. For a future comedian, I had dreadful timing.

Another time I asked her to go to a movie and she replied, 'I'm leaving for Africa tomorrow.'

'I think you're overreacting', I replied. 'I wasn't asking for marriage, only *Terminator 2*.' But she really was going to South Africa, to represent our university at an international debating tournament. The day after she arrived home I went over to visit and brought my guitar.

'What's the guitar for?' she asked.

I channelled the soul of a tortured poet and sang the deepest and most meaningful version of Leonard Cohen's 'Suzanne' for her. I stared into her gorgeous blue eyes and there was just the briefest flicker of a moment when I was positive that she knew we were meant to be.

'That's beautiful, Anh.' And I got a kiss on the cheek.

Damn. Still 'just friends'. Bloody hell, this girl was tough. It took ages to learn that song. *Stupid Leonard Cohen and his sharp minor seventh chords. Who writes songs with sharp minor sevenths in them? What more did I need to do? Surely she knew I adored her. I mean, I don't learn songs for any of my other friends. I've never sung a soulful ballad to Phil or Lloydy.*

But it didn't matter. She still had no desire to date this Vietnamese, football-playing palm reader.

One morning I needed to go to the shops and Khoa and Tram were coming with me. Khoa needed to buy some hair gel, and Tram just liked to go shopping. I was getting impatient waiting.

'Come on, guys.'

Khoa is a paradox. Most of the time he has no problem wearing his pyjamas and a footy jumper down to the supermarket, but every now and then, when he decides he needs to look good, you can put money on having to wait for him. This morning in particular, Khoa was taking ages, and Tram wasn't ready either, so I left them both at home and went by myself.

After driving less than a block up the road I stopped to turn right. A couple of cars were coming in the opposite direction, and I was waiting for them to pass. I had been stopped for maybe four or five seconds when something caught my eye in the rear-view mirror. I didn't even have time to see what it was when there was a colossal *BANG!* I suddenly found myself twenty metres up the road in a mangled mess of steel. A bus had run into me. The driver turned out to be an old man who didn't even see my stopped car. A policeman told me later, after they'd examined the tyre marks, that he was charging along full pelt like Sandra Bullock in *Speed*.

As I was sitting in the driver's seat covered in glass, a strange calmness came over me and a weird footy instinct kicked in. Every now and then in rugby league you get smacked so hard by a big guy that you find yourself lying flat on the ground staring at the sky. You always get back up slowly, going through a routine, one by one moving each limb to see if you're okay. Arms working? Check. Legs moving? Check. Neck and head still joined? Check. And I did this after the accident. Amazingly, after being hit by a speeding bus, I was a hundred per cent unscathed. Not a scratch.

The car, on the other hand, didn't do so well. My Nissan Pulsar was half its size, squashed up like an accordion, with the back seats crushed right up against the front. All I could think was, *Thank god Tram and Khoa didn't come, one of them would've been killed.* I went to open the door to get out. It was jammed. By this stage there were strangers running towards me from the outside. A man helped pull me through the broken window. Just then I saw my mum running towards the car screaming her lungs out. What a sight it must have been for her. To hear this enormous bang, come out the front of the house, and see that a bus had swallowed up the hatchback her son was driving.

'Mum, Mum, I'm okay!' I called out.

She came up and hugged me. She started running through her own version of my footy routine and grabbed my arms and shook them around, inspected the back of my head, my neck, my legs, handling me roughly like I was some sort of gladiator slave she was about to purchase, all the while catching her breath and uttering, 'thankyougod . . . thankyougod . . . thankyougod . . .'

As sirens approached, everything settled down, and after Mum was a hundred per cent sure her boy was indeed unscathed, she noticed the old bus driver sitting on the footpath. He looked a mess. Sitting there, his face was as white as a sheet, his head was looking down at his trembling hands. He was still holding the bus keys but his hands were shaking so much that they jingled loudly.

Mum walked over, sat down beside him, put her arm around him and said, 'My son okay. No worry.' I realised she was trying to comfort a scared old man, and my heart filled with love for her.

The bus company took a few months to process all the paperwork, but soon its insurance people confirmed it was going to pay us $4000 for the Pulsar. We jumped for joy because we only paid three and a half for it, and that had been years earlier.

'Four grand! Anh, let a bus run you over once a week. We'll be rich!' Khoa hollered. Tram whacked him on the back of the head.

It might seem a strange way to react to an accident, but Khoa, Tram and I really were absolutely overjoyed that I had been hit by a bus. Suddenly there was money, lots of money, more money than we'd seen for a long, long time. We all knew exactly how to spend it. Up to this point in our lives we had never owned a computer. But around this time, in western society at least, computers were quickly moving from being a luxury to a necessity and all three of us were desperate to get one.

Many of my university assignments had to be typed, and hand-written ones were actually given an automatic 10 per cent deduction in marks. So everyone handed in typed assignments except for me. It was fine for a while, as I usually scored high enough that even with 10 per cent off I was still way clear of the 50 per cent pass mark. But as I got more and more disenchanted with law and attended less and less classes, I was starting to sail much closer to the line.

We went shopping and the cheapest computer we could find, with the necessary printer, monitor, hard drives, software, etc., etc., was $3750. That's how much a basic PC cost back then. I spent the remaining $250 on a Toyota Corona and we were all happy.

The computer turned out to be very significant, with Khoa and I both writing our first screenplays on its Honeywell keyboard. Still to this day Khoa likes to mention the very lucky day when a bus driver almost killed Anh and kick started his movie career.

In my second year of university, I was juggling lots of balls: law and art, helping Mum out with the garments, working at a cake shop and a bunch of other odd jobs, doing anything to earn extra cash. One of the more interesting positions I got was working at Australia Post as a mail sorter. I thought you'd just apply and that'd be it. Easy. But to get the job I had to pass a postcode test, which meant I had to learn off-by-heart all the postcodes of every single suburb in New South Wales in one week.

It was one of those tasks that seemed just about impossible when you start out, but the brain is an amazing machine. Pretty soon I was confident enough to attempt the test. I had to sit down at a table with a wall of small pigeonholes in front of me. A woman timed me with a stopwatch and when she said 'Go', I picked up a stack of test envelopes with addresses on them and started slinging them into the correct slots.

It was a hellish ride, especially if I got stuck on one—there are some bloody obscure suburbs out there. *Llandilo? Oh my god, is it 2474 or 2747?* Once I'd finished off that stack, I picked up more. Ten minutes later 'Time's up' was called. The woman came over and spent a few minutes checking to see if I'd sorted them correctly. It was a very nervous wait; if I failed I'd just spent a week learning postcodes for nothing.

'Anh Do? Pass.'

Whoo-hoo!

For a few months every year, especially around Christmas when it got busy, the post office would call me up and off I'd go to do my eight hours of sorting mail. I was a casual worker so the only shifts available were night ones. I'd clock in at 10 p.m. and then clock out at 6 the following morning.

I learned a valuable lesson about night shifts in that job: your body never really gets used to it. I'd try to sleep during the day, but the sun always managed to bully its way through the tiniest crack in my metal blinds. I did manage to catch a few naps here and there, but it was hard to string a solid six hours together. I was always exhausted by about 1 a.m. From then on I'd stare up at the clock every thirty minutes or so, until an old Vietnamese guy called Minh, who had been an engineer in Vietnam before the war but was now a permanent mail sorter, took me under his wing.

'Anh, you got to stop looking at the clock so often, it makes the time go slower.'

Minh had also escaped Vietnam as a refugee, leaving his family behind with a view to sponsoring them to come over later, but he got stuck in a refugee camp in the Philippines for seven years. By the time he got to Australia his wife had found a new husband to help care for the two young kids she had to feed. It broke Minh's heart. Minh decided he'd help me get into the groove of sorting mail.

'Anh, watch me.'

Some people just seem to do 'their thing' effortlessly. He started showing me, sorting mail at an incredible pace, a rhythm that seemed so easy. He finished the stack, slowly but mindfully picked up another, and then the rhythmic motion would kick in all over again. It was like he was in a meditative state as his hand automatically flicked envelopes into their correct slots.

'You get into it, forget about time, and you will know it's nearly morning when you hear the birds.' And Minh was right. Around about 5 a.m. I did start hearing the chirping of birds. I then looked up at the industrial windows way up under the factory roof and saw a gentle glow of blue. That was when I got a second wind because I knew I was nearly there.

As boring as the work was, I was happy to have the job, which often called me in on weekends and that meant time-and-a-half or even double-time pay. The job had one other fringe benefit too. For years afterwards my knowledge of postcodes was a very cool party trick. I'd be at the university bar having a conversation with some girls: 'So what suburb do you live in?'

'Mosman.'

'That's 2088.'

'How'd you know that?'

'I just know. What about you?'

'Croydon.'

'2132.'

'Oh my god, are you like a genius savant or something?'

'No, but I can do a few cool things . . . you haven't locked your keys in your car have you?'

I was old enough now to earn legitimate money and it was a wonderful newfound freedom for my bank balance to no longer rely on the fickle libido of my Siamese fighting fish. Mum was sewing seven days a week, I had my several jobs and even Khoa, at sixteen, had got a job in a printing factory. We worked and worked and eventually scrimped and saved up a decent amount of money. Then Mum borrowed another chunk of cash from family and friends and it was time to go shopping.

Mum had heard about three brand-spanking-new industrial-strength sewing machines that were being sold at cost price. They were fifteen thousand in total. We bought them and set them up in the back garage of the house in Yagoona. Mum was thrilled, she finally had proper machines and was going to be able to get us ahead with a bit more hard work. Things were looking up!

One day about three months later, I was eating my breakfast when Mum came running in the back door.

'What's happened to the sewing machines?'

'What are you talking about?'

'The machines, they're gone!'

I ran out the back and sure enough, our sewing machines had been stolen during the night.

I was angry, but Mum was absolutely shattered. She had saved up for years, and still owed money on those machines. The next month was desperately hard. My mum is an incredibly positive person but when those bastards took away the machines, they took away the opportunity for her to finally give her kids a better life. She tried to hide her pain but we could see it. That night I couldn't sleep. I woke up to get a glass of water and I heard Mum crying gently in her bedroom.

I went back to bed and stared at the ceiling for hours, I just couldn't fall asleep. Eventually I got up and went out to the park at the front of our house and lay in the middle of the field, in complete darkness, until 3 a.m. in the morning. I was cursing everyone and everything for my mother's suffering. Most of all I cursed my father. He should've been there to protect us. I decided then and there that I was going to find the prick and make him pay.

The next day I walked to the public phone up the road. I didn't want to call from home because I didn't want anyone in my family to know I was trying to get in touch with my Dad. I phoned Uncle Eight and asked him where Dad was.

'He's living in Melbourne these days. You didn't know that?'

'No, I didn't.'

'Do you have his number?'

'No, I don't.'

'All right, I'll go get it.'

I waited for what seemed like a very long time, although in reality it was probably only a couple of minutes, for Uncle Eight to come back with the phone number for me. I scribbled it down on a Franklins shop-a-docket, in between the half-price dry cleaning and the twenty-per-cent-off Fruitworld offer.

'Thanks, Uncle Eight. You been well?'

'Yeah. You? How's your mum?'

'Good, good', I muttered. It was a strange conversation with a man who used to live with us and had looked after me like I was his own son. After Dad left we had very little contact with his side of the family, and I'd lost touch with all these uncles I'd known so well. I felt like asking him if he'd swallowed any more jewellery lately. Instead I mumbled, 'All right then, see you later'.

I hung up and stuck the docket in my wallet. It sat there for a month. What was I waiting for? Nothing really, just procrastinating.

One Sunday morning I walked up the road again and dialled the number. *Bringggg-bringggg, bringggg-bringggg.* I heard someone pick up on the other end and a male voice said ''Ello' but it sounded Mediteranean. *What the hell? Who turned my dad into Stavros the Greek?*

I looked down at the number. *Bugger, I forgot to put the '03' area code in first.* I hung up and stuck the docket back in my wallet. Where it stayed for another two years.

I loved studying art so much I signed up for extra drawing classes at the local community college. After the first session the teacher asked if anyone lived in the Bankstown region because a few people in the class needed a lift home. I put up my hand and was introduced to a girl named Rachel. Over the next eight weeks I gave her a lift home and soon we started going out.

Rachel was a redhead and she rode a motorbike, it was awesome—like dating the girl off the matchbox. Rachel and I used to like going to outdoor markets and one day we were at the ones in Bondi and I was looking around for a stall to buy her a crystal necklace. Amethyst is the crystal of tranquillity and Rachel was a fiery redhead who could have done with a bit of calming down. We searched everywhere, and I was surprised to find that there weren't any. *Geez. What sort of self-respecting full-of-dodgy-hippies market doesn't sell crystals?*

My fish breeding had taught me about supply and demand. I told Rachel that this kind of stuff would do well here. It was the perfect little gifty thing that was cheap and could be taken home by people who were just spending a day at the beach.

'If I had the cash to start a stall, I could make a killing here.'

'Why don't we?' she said.

'I don't have the capital.'

'I do.'

And with those two little words, Rachel and I became partners in a market stall business.

The agreement was that I would run the stall and Rachel would be the financier. It went ballistic, the crystals flying off the trestle table faster than kebabs outside the footy. The only problem with having a monopoly and raking it in, was that soon other entrepreneurial hippies noticed. Within a few months there were five other stalls selling crystals and crystal jewellery. My market dominance was crumbling and I needed an edge.

One day Rachel and I watched *Dances with Wolves* and I had an idea. *This is it!* I expanded to authentic American Indian souvenirs, which were imported from the United States. Tomahawks, headdresses, jewellery and axes—a natural, logical fit for English backpackers at Australia's Bondi Beach. The stuff was so 'in' at the time and it went berserk. Pretty soon I had two girls running stalls for me. I was managing a franchise, and making good money out of it.

One day I had a tomahawk worth $200 for sale. A lady came up and asked me, straight up: 'Are you American Indian?'

'Actually, I'm from Vietnam', I told her. She smiled.

'Well, you look very much like an American Indian.'

'Well, thanks . . . I guess', I replied. She bought the tomahawk, so I got the money as well as the comment.

As soon as she left, I found a mirror to see if I could see what she saw. *The eyes? No. The nose? I don't think so. It must be the hair.* By this time I had grown my mullet out and it had turned into a shiny, black, off-the-shoulder mane.

A week later, a guy came along and asked, 'What native tribe are you from?' This time I thought, *He wants a native, I'll give him a native.*

I had heard about an Indian tribe called the Chippewa, so I told him proudly, 'Actually, my grandfather's Chippewa'. He had already bought a tomahawk, and he was happy. But it made his day that he had bought it from a genuine Chippewa, via Vietnam.

After a while it became obvious that Rachel and I didn't actually have that much in common. We would talk about a few superficial things and then run out of things to say. It didn't matter how good she looked on that bike, we were at the beginning of the end of our relationship. In the way that it does when things start to break down, it actually started to annoy me that she was so nice and complimentary all the time.

'You're a really smart guy', she would keep saying. Well, everyone was good with their brain at university, that's how we got there. But Rachel was from a different world. I would say something simple, like, 'The sun was a beautiful colour when it set today'.

'Wow, you're so smart', she'd say.

One day I bought her a nice bracelet.

'Wow, this is so nice Anh . . . it must've been expensive.'

'Yeah it was. I had to sell a kidney.'

'Oh my god, did it hurt?'

I never forgot, however, that Rachel was always kind to me, that she'd put her faith in me when we started up the business, virtually handing me all her savings.

'You take care of it, Anh. You're the one with the business brain.'

When we finally broke up I felt indebted and paid her back all the profits we had amassed to date. She made triple her money back.

I called up Suzie one day and after some small talk I asked, 'You still with your boyfriend?'

'Yep. You still with your girlfriend?' I wasn't, but Suzie had just said 'yes' so I wasn't going to be outdone.

'Yeah, still with Rachel. Going strong, actually. She's great . . . really clever girl.'

The timing was off yet again; it was time to move on.

During my studying art phase I got into the whole alternative life-style . . . I began not only creating art on canvas but wearing things to decorate myself. I had hair that went all the way down to my lower back, the flannelette shirts gave way to seventies purple paisley ones I picked up from St Vinnies, and the thongs were thrown out to be replaced by pointy Bob Dylan-style boots. Before you knew it I had become a fully-fledged Vietnamese hippy.

I moved to Leura in the Blue Mountains, lived with two hippie girls and went with them to alternative music and folk festivals. I was trying to find out who I was, and tried all sorts of creative outlets. I played guitar, wrote a few songs, as well as studying law, and painting.

One hot December I headed off to a festival called Confest, an annual event that was described as Australia's largest outdoor alternative lifestyle festival. It was hilarious; eight hundred hairy, smelly, tie-dyed hippies turning a riverside camping ground into a commune.

I was running fire-twirling classes. I'd learned how to fire twirl at the Bondi markets when I was selling the Native American artefacts. There was a guy at a store next to us flogging funny hats, juggling batons, and five-foot-long sticks which had a Kevlar wick on each end . . . 'fire sticks'. In the downtime he taught me how to twirl these and I picked it up quickly.

I had just finished a class when a girl came up and asked me for directions. She had short dark hair, a milky white complexion and a mesmerising English accent. There must've been something about this fire spinning Oriental Tonto that was attractive, because we exchanged phone numbers and soon we started dating.

Juliette was a psychology student who was a bit older than me and had a penchant for quoting Gandhi or Joan of Arc mid-sentence. Every now and then she'd confidently pull out a line that could've been from a famous moment in history . . . or a Hallmark card. It was hard to tell. It didn't matter, her accent made it sound official.

We would spend hours just hanging out discussing the meaning of existence and trying to solve mankind's greatest dilemmas. Juliette liked lending me big books on politics and history and eagerly awaited my finishing the book so that we could together scrutinise the states of mind of iconic leaders. She would be disappointed if I hadn't read the book. It felt a bit like homework but she was worth it.

Juliette also had very strong convictions and wanted to do something about everything in the world she thought was a problem. For example, she was vegan and wanted me to turn vegan too. At first I didn't even know what it meant.

'Is that like vegetarian?'

'Yes, but a wee tad different. Vegetarians eat cheese and eggs and drink milk, but I don't eat any animal products at all. I just don't think it's right.'

'Okay then, if you feel that strongly about it, from today onwards I too shall be vegan!'

We stopped at the service station and I came back with an Aeroplane Jelly.

'You can't eat that Anh.'

'Why not?'

'Because jelly is made from animal hooves.'

'Really? No way. I had no idea.' The Aeroplane Jelly went straight in the bin.

'How about chocolates then?'

'Sorry. It's got milk.'

'How about custard?'

'Got eggs.'

'How 'bout oysters?'

'Of course not, Anh!'

'C'mon, Juliette. I can understand that you love animals and you don't want them killed, but horses' hooves are just like our finger-nails—doesn't hurt at all when you cut them off!' I drifted off for a second with this weird theme song in my head:

I like fingernail jelly.
Fingernail jelly for me.
I like it for dinner, I like it for . . .

'Anh, I'm serious.'

'Sure, I'll do it.'

I liked making an effort with girlfriends, it was my father's streak. But if we ever went to a fancy restaurant, Juliette would sit down, question everything on the menu and eliminate every single dish! So there we'd be, dressed up nice, bottle of wine, views of the Sydney Opera House, and for dinner the waiter brings over . . .

'Steamed vegetables for madam and for sir.'

I felt like I should have booked a table for two at the local Fruitworld. After all, in my wallet I did still have that shop-a-docket.

I didn't realise what an impact the vegan lifestyle would have on me. For a start, I dropped from about eighty kilograms down to sixty-eight. At the time I was playing rugby league, and I was the captain of my team and was supposed to set an example on the field. But being vegan meant my example was to get absolutely hammered every time I went in to make a tackle. I thought my body was still the same, and so I would go in thinking I was still eighty kilos, but I would just bounce off the runners like a weedy ten-year-old kid.

Juliette also liked to psychoanalyse me. I'd make a simple comment like, 'Geez I'm hungry.' And she would say, 'You're not hungry Anh, that hunger you *think* you feel is just a yearning that stems from your abandonment issues.'

About six months into the relationship I noticed that the books Juliette was lending me were getting thicker and more boring, so I'd just read a couple of bits near the end and then pretend I'd finished it. She caught me out one day and put it down to my 'lack of commitment issues leading to an inability to complete anything of significance'.

The afternoon after we split up I went to a pub and ordered a Surf and Turf consisting of a half-kilo steak topped with four monster prawns of significant size and absolutely completed every morsel. Best meal of my life!

Most guys turn to their male friends for advice about women; my go-to guy was a girl—Suzie. When things were on the rocks with Juliette, I went home and called Suzie, who'd been lending me books, CDs and all sorts of things since we'd become friends years ago.

'You know how you lent me that poetry book by that German guy, Goethe,' I said sheepishly.

'Yep, what do you think?' she asked.

'It's kinda boring, so I haven't been reading it,' I fessed up.

'That's cool,' she replied.

There was a slight pause and then Suzie continued:

'You know how you lent me that special edition *Mad* magazine?'

'Yep, what do you think?' I asked.

'It's kinda boring, so I haven't been reading it.'

'Ha! We're even then. See you at uni tomorrow.'

Suzie even helped out with my car on occasion. The old canary yellow Corona I'd bought after the bus hit me lived down to its $250 price tag. It was unreliable. It could lurch around the city at low speed but you couldn't trust it to go long distances. And it was easy to break into.

The car was useful, however, to get me around the various weekend markets in Sydney. Although Rachel and I had broken up, I was still running the business, selling crystals, Native American artefacts, candles and the like. One Saturday, I had a stall outside Hornsby Westfield in Sydney's north, and at the end of the day I had $5000 worth of goods that needed to be put away somewhere safe. The problem was that I was going to a party on the Hawkesbury River with my current girlfriend, and the Corona wasn't reliable enough to drive all the way, nor was it safe enough to leave parked on a street chock-full of jewellery. We decided to catch a train, which meant I needed to find somewhere secure to leave the car.

The only person I knew who lived near Hornsby railway station was Suzie, whose family lived on a large block in the affluent suburb of Wahroonga. A few hours before the train was scheduled to leave, I rang her.

'It's Anh. Can I leave my car in your big driveway?'

'Sure.'

Suzie's family knew me pretty well. They enjoyed seeing my different phases and fads. I parked in the middle of her family's very long driveway and was greeted at the door by her brother.

'Anh's at the door,' he said, then whispered inside to the family, 'Come and see. Quick.'

First they were wondering, *What five-dollar rust bucket is he driving now?* They were used to my bad cars over the years. I picked Suzie up in them. One of the first times we hung out together, I drove up in a car whose bumper bar fell off as it approached the house. Nothing says 'potential good boyfriend for daughter' like, 'Hi, Mrs Fletcher. Nice to meet you. Can I borrow a coat hanger?'

Suzie walked out to find me fiddling with the coat hanger and some duct tape, trying to reattach the bumper bar to the car. Her father appeared with a set of pliers.

'Thanks, Mr Fletcher,' I said, embarrassed. Soon the bumper bar was happily reunited with the chassis.

Anyway, on this occasion the Corona still had its bumper bar firmly attached, but just as Suzie peered into it, a young girl emerged from the passenger's side. She wore no shoes and she had underarm hair and feathers hanging out of her three-foot-long dreadlocks. She wore a multi-coloured skirt that was in a bright Aztec design. I was dressed up the same way. We were quite a sight.

'Thanks, Mr and Mrs Fletcher. I really appreciate you letting me leave the car here tonight. I'll come back and pick it up in the morning, on my way to my stall in Hornsby.'

Her parents didn't bat an eyelid as they waved us goodbye and we went off to our party. Inside the house, I later learned, the family went into hysterics.

'Has Anh joined the circus?' her mother asked.

'No. That's just how he dresses these days!'

HAHAHAHAHAHAHA!

• Nine •

Suzie and I were in a lot of classes together at uni and we were still just friends, hanging out in the same group and teasing each other in class like five years olds. One year the university camping club ran a trek, which I went on with a couple of mates from our class. The expedition was in the Moreton National Park near Canberra, in the middle of winter. It was freezing.

There was a convoy of two vehicles and, after a long drive, the car I was in got separated from the other one. When we arrived we parked the four-wheel drive and trekked for a while, but it got dark and pretty soon we just had to make camp where we were and meet up with the others in the morning. My backpack and all my gear were in the other car. Lucky my mate Steve had a two-man tent. As night arrived it was getting colder and colder and it dawned on me I didn't have a sleeping bag. So Steve lent me all his warm clothes. I put on as many layers as I could, but I was still freezing—the kind of cold you feel deep in your bones; it makes your teeth chatter so much your whole brain starts vibrating.

I got up and started doing sit-ups to try and warm myself; *thirty-five, thirty-six* . . . I was getting tired, my abs were hurting like there was a knife in them, and still I was freezing. Steve, he was snug in his sleeping bag.

'Just come in with me', he said. I looked at the one-man sleeping bag and figured it would be quite a tight squeeze for two blokes.

'No, I'm okay.' I turned over and started doing push-ups.

'All right, but if you get cold, we can share.' Then Steve went to sleep.

I finished forty push-ups and it brought me a temporary warmth that lasted a whole minute and a half. Then I was freezing again. I lay there trying to will myself warm, thinking of everything I could that would warm me up—fires, hot sand at Bondi Beach, my brother's great big polyester blanket with the horse printed on it. None of this worked and after another thirty minutes I figured I would die from hypothermia.

'Hey, S-S-S-Steve.' Nothing. He was fast asleep. I tapped him on the shoulder and woke him up.

'Hey, Steve. M-m-m-maybe we c-can undo the sleeping bag and we can b-both use it like a blanket.'

'All right.'

Steve unzipped the sleeping bag and we lay side by side, making sure there was a good gap between us. Halfway through the night, I woke up and discovered I was spooning Steve like a favourite lover.

'Steve?'

'Yeah?'

'Ahh, I think I'm cuddling you . . .' We both pulled away.

Five freezing minutes later . . .

'Anh, you still cold?'

'Yeah. You?'

'Yeah. How about we just not tell anyone?'

'Awesome!'

We nudged closer to each other until there was body contact, and lay side by side, enjoying the purely platonic heat emanating from the other guy's body.

'We won't tell anyone, right?' I checked.

'Course not'

The next morning the other car turned up, I got my own sleeping bag and the rest of the camping trip was uneventful. On Monday morning, at our first class at uni, Steve walked in and announced to the room: 'Guess what happened on our camping trip?' and proceeded to tell the whole class about me pestering him to get the cuddle on.

'Anh's gay', the boys began to yell.

Suzie piped up: 'No he's not.'

Wow! I was stunned. *What's Suzie saying here? She's asserting my hetero–ness?*

'Anh's not good looking enough to be gay', she said, grinning.

I went with Steve and some other uni mates one night to watch stand-up comedy at the Harold Park Hotel, which back then was a comedy institution. It had been running for years and was famous for being the venue where many of Australia's best comics started, and also the occasional 'drop in' from internationals, like Robin Williams.

On this particular night there wasn't anyone famous, it was cheap Monday, open mic night. Open mic is where aspiring and amateur comedians get to go on stage and do a five-or-so-minute routine. Sometimes you get good amateurs and sometimes you don't. On this occasion most of them weren't so good.

Halfway through one guy's attempt Steve turned to me and said, 'Anh, you're funnier than this guy.'

'No I'm not', I said, but in my head I went, *I reckon I am.*

The next time we went to open mic night I signed up to do a short routine. I told a yarn about a disastrous holiday I once went on and it went over really well. I was so surprised. It was a complete and utter fluke! I'd told the story a thousand times before to friends, and I knew it off-by-heart, so when I got up on stage, despite my trembling nerves, my familiarity with the story got me through.

Perhaps it was fate or destiny, but I got lucky that very night because there was a woman standing at the back of the room watching the show and she came up to me afterwards.

'Have you got ten minutes? I'm running a comedy room in Kings Cross', she said. 'If you're interested, I could book you for next week.' My face lit up then my stomach started whirling. As I walked away, I realised I had only three minutes' worth of material and I needed another seven.

I was in my fourth year of my five-year degree. Every year for students at that level there was a headhunting ritual in which the top firms conducted interviews early to snap up the best talent before graduation. I had every intention of finishing university, so even though I didn't like it, it seemed like I was well on my way to becoming a 'suit'.

I interviewed with many of the big companies—UBS Warburg, Macquarie Bank, Andersen Consulting, and others at that level. Of all these companies, Andersen had the most ridiculously intense recruitment process. First you sent in your resume, from which they culled out most applicants. Then you went through two rounds of interviews. More culling. Then the last hurdle was a three-day 'recruitment' retreat.

It was a hellishly intimidating experience. You were in a job interview for three whole days, knowing you were being watched while you ate, slept and showered—okay, maybe not while you slept, that'd be weird. You knew that out of the hundred or so candidates, only twenty were going to get job offers and the rest would get the 'Don't call us, we'll call you'.

It was at this retreat, with ninety-nine others jostling for attention and trying to out-do each other, that I realised once and for all that I didn't want to be in this environment. I really hated it. I'm sure

Khoa and me in our school uniforms.

The boys are growing up. This was my long-haired period.

Khoa and me on the set of *Footy Legends*. I trained pretty hard for six months to try to look like a football player.

Suzie. The girl with the smile that lights up my life.

Suzie and me at our wedding, with Suzie's parents, Robert and Frances Fletcher.

Suzie took these two photos of me when she was studying photography. This is one with me and Rocky the budgie.

Just swinging around.

Me and Phil. Still best mates.

I sketched this self portrait whilst studying art at TAFE.

Early stand-up comedy photo when I used to wear a flannelette shirt.

Dad with my son Xavier. Dad is healthy.

Mum and her three gorgeous grandsons.

Luda and me backstage on *Dancing with the Stars*. (Courtesy of Network 7)

Dancing with the Stars. Halfway through the season I dressed up as a soldier and dedicated the dance to my grand–mother. (Courtesy of Network 7)

Deal or No Deal. What a moment. (Courtesy of Network 7)

Our happy family at my third boy Leon's christening.

Uncle Huy, once a prisoner in a 're-education' camp, is the priest at Xavier's christening.

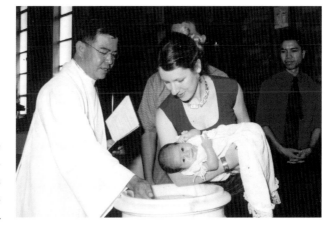

My darling wife and her boys being funny.

Mum and Luc on the river. At four years old Luc is already steering.

Me and the boys on the river. (L to r) Leon, Luc and Xavier.

My boys. My greatest joy.

Our big smiling family.

they were nice people, but the competitive nature of the whole thing made everyone seem so damn fake. Candidates were stealing ideas, feigning friendships, doing everything they could to stand out from the rest of the pack at all costs.

After it was over, I got a call up for the final interview with Andersen Consulting, the one where they basically tell you you had a job. So I'm sitting in this huge, cold, intimidating office and the guy reached across and said, 'Congratulations Anh, you've got the job'.

Whoo-hoooo!

'Any questions?'

I was going to let it slide, but I really wanted to know: 'How many hours a week do you work?'

It was a risky question to ask, and I'd waited till after finding out I had the job to ask it. If I'd asked too early, I might have sounded like I was a lazy bugger.

'Well, Anh, at my level, I'm doing about sixty to sixty-five hours a week. I'm trying to cut back, but it can get pretty intense.'

Holy Schmoly. It was a lot of hours to be doing something I knew I wouldn't like.

I walked away from the meeting in two minds. On the one hand I wanted to jump for joy; I knew my family would never be poor again—I'd just gotten a job that paid well enough for us to live a much better life. On the other hand I knew I was going to hate it.

That night I was booked in to do a comedy gig at a club. It went well and after the show I went up to another comic who had been around the traps, Dave Grant, and asked him how many hours a week he worked.

'Four.'

'Four?'

'Yeah, four. If it's a big week, maybe five, six hours tops.'

Dave was what you'd call a headline comedian—a professional who made a regular living out of doing stand-up. He was a bit of a legend on the circuit, an all-round nice guy who had mentored many young comedians.

'Around how much money do you guys make?' I then asked.

He gave me a range; professionals started at fifty to sixty thousand a year, some made a hundred thousand, and the big boys made whatever they wanted. But for an average headline comic, the salary was between fifty and hundred thousand. A light went on in my brain: That's more than Andersen Consulting was asking me to do for a sixty-hour week. *That's it*, I thought. *I'm going to switch.*

Of course, Dave forgot to tell me that it took the average comedian between five to ten years to become a headliner. He also forgot to tell me that many comedians spent years doing hundred-dollar gigs, so earning just a couple of hundred dollars a week. But something inside of me said, *This is frightening, but it's the right thing to do.*

I remember my father always said to me as a kid, 'When you know it's right for you, but it scares you, it means you have the most to gain from doing it'. I figured I would at least give it a crack and if it didn't work out, I could always go back to being a suit. When I told Andersen Consulting that I was going to have a go at being a stand-up comedian for a year, they said to me, 'Anh, if it doesn't work out, you've still got a job here with us if you want'.

And then it was time to tell Mum. Most kids would be worried about announcing to their single mum; 'Mum, after five years of university and a big job offer that will guarantee money and security for many years to come, I'm going to chuck it all in for a shot at becoming a stand-up comedian'.

'What's a stand-up comedian?' she asked.

There are no stand-up comedians in Vietnam. Sure there are comedies, but these consist of a troop of actors performing a comedy play. The thought of just one person on stage with a microphone making people laugh for an hour seemed like a ridiculous way to make a living.

'You think you can do it?' Mum asked.

'Yeah I think so. Anyway, Andersen said that if it doesn't work out, I can always go back and work for them.'

'All right. If you think you can do it, go for it.'

I love my mum. She's so damn optimistic and has so much faith in her children that sometimes I wonder whether we deserve it.

Now all I had to do was try and become a professional comedian in a year. I had a lot of motivation and a mother's blessing. A mother who was happy to continue spending long hours slaving away at a sewing machine so her son could have a shot at making a living out of a job she didn't even realise existed.

I worked like I was possessed. Any club that would have amateurs, I would sign up for, and so I was doing six or seven gigs a week. Some nights I'd do two gigs—I'd finish one then drive to another. In between I'd be writing and re-writing material, trying to improve the jokes, the material, the routine.

I was doing gigs for free, for $50, $20, a slab of beer, a cheese-burger—anything really. I took jobs that weren't even comedy, but if it entailed me getting up with a microphone, I was there. And where I could, I would mix comedy into the announcements. I was an MC at boxing tournaments, spruiked fruit and vegies in the mall, even performing magic tricks at kids' parties.

I asked around for tips and advice from the senior guys and Dave told me to do the hard gigs as they made you stronger. So one day I found myself in front of fifty bikers who were waiting for strippers to come on. It was a very, very hard gig, but it taught me how to be very funny very fast.

The following week I performed in front of twenty priests. I thought the bikers were hard, at least they laughed. The priests just looked at me blankly. When I finished I asked, 'What do I get for the gig?'

'Ten thousand Hail Marys.'

I worked as much as I could and it paid off. In 1999, about a year after I'd started doing comedy, I won the prestigious Harold

Park Hotel's Comedian of the Year award. I was one of the youngest comedians to ever win it and it was the launch pad that I needed. My friend and mentor Dave was one of the first to congratulate me.

I entered lots of comedy competitions in the beginning. One of the ones that meant the most to me was a competition in Canberra called Green Faces. It was a big national event that ran over ten weeks. They flew in comedians from all over the country and put them through early rounds, semi-finals and then the big grand final. The winner received $5000 in cash. I made the grand final, and I had a very good reason to want to win.

My little sister Tram rarely smiled for many years of her childhood. She had a number of dental problems that caused her top row of teeth to become all jammed up and lopsided. She was so embarassed that in every family photo she always had her lips shut tight. It wasn't anything a few years' worth of braces couldn't fix, but we just didn't have the money. So Tram went around feeling very self-conscious. She was hitting her late teens and her teeth in particular began to affect her confidence and self-esteem. So I was doing it for Tram.

There were ten finalists altogether and we were all very good; after all, we had just beaten everyone else from our own state. I felt awfully nervous because in getting to the grand final I had used up all my best material; I only had my B-grade stuff left. I was furious at myself for not saving some of the good jokes in case I got to the final. Here was the biggest moment of my life so far and I had no good gags left.

It turned out I wasn't the only one who had used up all my best jokes; all the others were in the same boat. The crowd was so pumped up, though, they enjoyed everyone anyway. At the end of the night the audience voted with a little sheet of paper and a pencil, just like a ballot, that was collected by the staff. Not long after the organisers announced third, then second, then first . . .

'And the winner is: Anh Do!'

Whoo-hoooo!

As soon as I got off stage I raced over to a payphone.

'Mum, I won!'

'Tram, Anh's won! Anh's won!' Mum screamed. It was a truly great moment in my life. Mum and Tram had stayed up to midnight awaiting the phone call and I was able to deliver them the news they had been hoping for.

The events manager, Mr Laing, walked over to me, lifted open my jacket and stuck a very, very fat envelope into my pocket— a much fatter envelope than the ones Mum used to give me to pay for my school fees. I had never held five thousand cash before, so when all the other guys went out drinking afterwards I was too nervous about getting mugged or dropping my winnings. I went straight back to the hotel room, double locked the door, and slept with the money under my pillow. I woke up the next morning and saw in the mirror that I had a huge, deep envelope-shaped indent on my cheek. It didn't matter, I'd won five thousand big ones, and Tram was going to get her teeth fixed. Tram is a gorgeous girl and now she has a beautiful smile.

One day I decided to call up Suzie out of the blue and she told me she had recently broken up with her boyfriend.

'Well, do you want to meet up after uni to have one of those coconut ice-creams we used to have?'

We met up and everything was going so well that after ice-cream we decided to go and see the film *42 Up*, the latest instalment of a documentary series by British director Michael Apted, where he revisits a group of English people every seven years to see what shape their lives have taken. The film made me realise that life flies by and you've really got to seize the moment. In fact it reminded me of my father's philosophy; 'There are only two times in life, there's now and there's too late'.

Afterwards we both were still a bit reluctant to go home so I suggested we have something to eat. We had dinner at a fancy restaurant in Darling Harbour. Later on, I went to the bathroom and on the way back I whispered in her ear, 'Okay, let's go.'

Suzie's eyes widened: 'What about the bill?'

'Just get up and start walking now.'

Suzie was so stunned she just followed me. Once we were out of the restaurant, we took off—running and laughing our way through the crowds and across Darling Harbour. Once we were back at the car, I fessed up: 'I paid the bill on the way back from the bathroom.'

She whacked me on the shoulder.

'Oh my god! I can't believe you did that!'

'I can't believe *you* did that. You didn't even try to go back and pay!'

Another whack.

We drove down to Clifton Gardens near Mosman and hung out at this beautiful bay, looking at the lights and stars and listening to the water lapping the shore. The temperature had dropped and it was getting cold, so I gave her a cuddle. I don't know what made me do it, maybe there was some magic in the air that night. I said to her, 'You know, all these years have gone by, but I think I'm still very much in love with you'. She gave me that smile.

We sat and talked all through the night until the morning. Just talked, nothing else. It was wonderful. Then she told me something.

'Anh, just a few weeks ago I said to my friend, "There's this guy called Anh and I think he might be the perfect person for me and I don't know why we're not a couple".'

I gave her an enormous hug and that's when we decided to be together.

The stand-up comedy was starting to take off and I began getting offered little comedy spots on TV, just five minutes of stand-up here and there on obscure late night shows. Then, round about a year and a half into my comedy career I got offered my first TV hosting role. It was on a show called *Rush TV*, a youth variety program aimed at sixteen to twenty-four year olds. The station ran it on Sunday mornings and it ended up becoming popular with late-night party animals who wanted something to help them get over their hangovers.

During my time hosting the show I got a phone call from a magazine called *Australian Women's Forum*. I had never heard of them but it sounded like just another glossy, like *Woman's Day* or *Women's Weekly*. They wanted to interview me, take a photo, do a big write-up.

'No problem.' When you're on a television show, you are obliged to do as much publicity as you can to develop a profile and ratings.

I told Brendan, my producer, about my busy publicity schedule.

'Next week I have to do the Melbourne *Age*, the *Sydney Morning Herald* and *Australian Women's Forum*.'

'*Women's Forum*? You sure?' Brendan asked.

'Yeah. Why?'

'You know it's women's porn, don't you?'

'No way, man.' I didn't even know women's porn existed. 'You're kidding aren't you?'

'It's women's porn. They make it sound all classy and call it "erotica", but it's like *Playboy* for ladies.' Brendan told me.

'I . . . They . . . They didn't mention anything like that.'

'Well, it could be just an ordinary photo with an article, nothing too risqué', he said. 'I'll check.' So he rang the magazine.

'Anh can take his shirt off if he wants to but we're not going to ask him to do anything he doesn't want to do', they confirmed to him.

'You can do it if you want. It's good exposure', he said.

I glared at him.

'Pardon the pun.'

Suzie thought it was the funniest thing ever, and my family also thought it was a joke.

'Why on earth would they want you?'

I decided I had to see for myself. I went into a newsagent far, far away from home, sneaking in wearing a hat and sunnies, to buy a copy. When I opened it up, there were nude men all through it. *This is not for me.* I rang the producers.

'I think I might not do this one.'

It turns out the producer who answered the phone was my least favourite of them, and quite a tough cookie.

'No, you've got to do it.'

'It's got naked men all through it. My mum likes to collect all the publicity I do and I don't think she'll like this one.'

'Get over yourself, Anh. Just do it.'

'Hang on a minute', I said. 'If *Playboy* wanted one of our female co-hosts to go in the magazine, you'd advise against it.'

'You're right. I would. But this is different, Anh. It's different for boys and girls. You have to do it for the show.'

I really was uncomfortable with it, and so I went straight over to Brendan who was the top-level producer and told him that I was going to have to be a pain this time, but I wasn't going to do it.

'Sweet, Anh. No worries at all.'

Phew. Throughout my career I've always heeded my mother's advice to me when I was a kid: 'To thine own self be true, Anh. Never let others force you into anything you don't want to do. Let your own integrity be the ultimate guide.'

At our next family gathering Suzie decided to tell everyone, and they all thought it was an absolute hoot and laughed their heads off. Uncle Dung, who had a big gut, no hair and several chins, piped up:

'What about me? Can't I do it instead? How much will they pay me?'

One of the best things about *Rush TV* was that it gave me a regular income which was written down on paper. Up to this point I had been desperate to get a bank loan to buy Mum a house. I'd tried once before but got knocked back. Now, armed with a TV contract, I went shopping for a place for all of us to live in. After a month of looking around I found a double-storey, four-bedroom, three-bathroom brick house in a cul-de-sac. It had a pool, sunken lounge and an enormous kitchen—an absolute prerequisite because my mum loves to cook and feed people. It was just perfect. The only problem was that there were several other families who thought it was perfect also, and were already making offers on the place. I called up the Century 21 woman and made her an offer that was as far as I could stretch.

'Yes, Anh, the owner will take your offer because he needs to sell asap, but I need you to sort it all out and come in tomorrow morning to sign the contract.'

Sweet. I went back to the bank, told them the price of the house and showed them my income. The bank manager stroked his chin, ummed and ahhed for a bit, then said yes . . . on one condition. I needed a letter from my employer to verify my income.

I drove into *Rush TV*, typed up a simple income letter and knocked on the door of the producer's office.

'Come in!'

The only producer who was around was the really difficult one that tried to force me to do the *Women's Forum* shoot.

'Hi Samantha. I'm buying a house and I just need your autograph on the bottom of this to say I'm earning what I'm earning.'

'You'll have to come back later. I'm busy.'

I looked over and she was just surfing the net, researching one of the stories we were filming later that week. Not an urgent task.

'I've only got half an hour to get this back to the bank and I just need ten seconds of your time to sign this Samantha.'

'I'm busy, Anh. Wait outside the door and I'll call you in when I'm done.'

'Okay. Sorry. I'll just be outside the door.'

So I waited. Twenty-nine minutes left to buy Mum a house. Twenty-eight minutes left. Twenty-seven... ten minutes left.

Just then the big head honcho of the company, the managing director, a gentleman by the name of Michael Duff, walked past.

'Anh, you're doing some great work for us, mate.'

'Thank you, sir.'

'You look a bit agitated. Something up?'

I was indeed agitated. I had a window of ten minutes left to get a signature on a bit of paper and achieve the greatest dream of my life. I told Mike the scenario. 'Geez, Anh, there's not much more important than that, mate. I'll write you a letter myself. Come into my office.'

Five minutes later Mike and I were faxing the letter to the bank, Mike got on the phone himself to reassure the bank manager and the next day I signed a contract to buy one of the finest houses in Yagoona for my dear mum. It was one of the best days of my life.

I remember taking Mum in to see the place. She walked in, took one look at the polished wooden floorboards and started crying. All she could mutter was, 'Beautiful, beautiful, beautiful'.

I took Suzie out to dinner one night and afterwards we strolled down to a park overlooking the harbour and hung out for a while watching boats and eating chocolates. Then right on the dot of 9 p.m., a guy with a huge bunch of flowers turned up and announced it was for 'The Most Beautiful Woman in the World'. He handed it to Suzie and she gave me a big hug and kiss. Luckily it was me who had organised it. A little awkward otherwise! I introduced Suzie to my mate Eden, who lived just up the road.

'Thanks, Edes', I said to him.

Suzie, being a polite girl, asked him, 'Do you want a chocolate, Eden, before you go?'

'Oh yeah', he replied. 'Lovely night isn't it?' He then took a seat next to me and started getting stuck into my box of Ferreros.

'Edes, don't you have to get back? You mentioned an assignment you had to do.'

'Nuh, I finished it. These chocolates are great, aren't they?'

Surely the idiot could tell we wanted to be alone. I put up with him for another couple of minutes.

'Eden, thanks for doing this for me, but why don't you go home before I head-butt the bridge of your nose.'

'Ahh, okay, see you later.'

He shoved a final chocolate in his mouth, then took another for the road before he disappeared into the darkness. I quietly wished that an escaped panther from the nearby zoo would jump out and eat him.

About three months into our relationship, Suzie and I were walking hand in hand along Ettalong Beach on the Central Coast and I knew I was deeply happy. I remember being captivated by the shafts of sunlight that pierced through the clouds and danced on the glassy water. I told Suzie it was like they were putting on a performance just for us.

All of a sudden there was an enormous boom of thunder, the clouds gave way and rain bucketed down. Suzie giggled and started running along the beach in the rain. The chase was on. I grabbed her, picked her up and looked down at this crazy, laughing, beautiful girl in my arms. Droplets of rain slipped down her perfect face.

I gently put her back on her feet and got down on one knee.

'You know you are my soul mate and I've always loved you. Will you marry me, Suzanne?'

She cried, I laughed, and we kissed. Then we both cried and laughed again. And it was done. There we were, crouched on the wet sand in the rain, laughing, cuddling and kissing; a boy and a girl who had just promised to be with each other for the rest of their lives.

'If you find the right woman, don't muck around and waste any time, marry her.' The advice of a father who'd pissed off many years ago.

When I was twelve years old we would sit as a family on the farm porch on a hot summer night. Khoa and I would be lying on the ground, letting the cold concrete cool our backs. Mum and Dad would be sitting on an old couch with Tram on Mum's knee. Dad would have one arm around Mum's shoulder, the other hand holding a beer. Mum would look up at the bright moon and recount stories of the old world.

'Your father used to love moonlit nights.'

'Why's that, Mum?'

''Cos it's easier to catch crickets when the moon's bright.' Catching crickets was one of the few pastimes my father and his brothers had growing up in a poor village.

'Your dad was the best catcher of crickets in the whole district.'

We'd heard this story countless times but we still loved it, so we asked the question we all knew he was waiting for: 'What was the secret, Dad?'

He grinned. 'They come out of their dirt hole . . . when you piss into it.'

Khoa, Tram and I would laugh like he had just told the best joke in the world.

'You don't like moonlit nights any more, do you?' Mum said as she ran her hand through my dad's thick, wobbly hair (which she loved to do).

'No', Dad said, going a bit quiet like he was remembering something. 'Moonlit nights were when they dropped the most bombs.'

He'd take a big gulp of beer, kiss Mum on the forehead and pull her closer. Then he'd turn to us and say, 'If you find the right woman, don't waste any time, marry her'.

When I was a kid and heard all these things Mum and Dad used to say, I never thought they'd stick with me. But here I was, twenty-two years old, newly engaged and I had this deep need to call my dad and say to him, 'Dad, I've found the right woman'.

Of course, I had lots of reasons not to tell the prick. But Suzie encouraged me to make contact.

'You still love him, Anh.'

'No I don't. Not anymore.'

One night I was sitting up late at night, unable to sleep. Those bloody crickets were so loud. I went out to my car, drove up the road to the payphone, got out the fading shop-a-docket that had been in my wallet for two years, and dialled the number.

'Hello', a raspy voice answered. I recognised it straight away.

'Dad, it's Anh.'

'Anh . . . hello, son.'

A silence followed for what seemed like four years.

'Anh?'

'I . . . I got your number from Uncle Eight. He told me you're living in Melbourne now.'

'I am living in Melbourne now.'

'What's your address?'

Within two minutes I was in the car driving to Melbourne.

It's incredibly difficult to describe the feelings that go on inside you when you're on your way to see a father you once adored, but for eight long years have been fantasising about killing. You play out the whole thing over and over again with different scenarios: a joyful reunion full of happy tears; an angry reunion where you knock him out. You drive and you cry and wipe the wet steering wheel with your flannelette shirt.

'What's the kid's name, Dad?'

'His name is Anh. I named him after you.'

That floored me. I looked at the little kid and he was the spitting image of my brother Khoa.

'He looks just like Khoa, aye?'

'He's just like Khoa', Dad said. Then he called the kid over.

'Come here, Fatty!'

He might've been named after me, but he got the nickname of my brother. When Khoa was a kid everyone called him 'Fatty'. Not to be cruel, it was just his nickname . . . because he was fat.

I played with Fatty Anh for a few minutes. He was a huge strong one-year-old and incredibly bright and cheeky. It was a welcome break from the tense conversation. I felt an urge to play with this kid who a part of me wanted to dislike; afterall I had always been incredibly protective of my brother Khoa and my sister Tram, and here's this strange kid from out of nowhere wanting to butt in on our territory. But on the other hand, the little tacker was hilarious and it was his resemblance to Khoa that took away any ill feeling that was desperately trying to surface.

I stayed for about an hour, mainly making small talk: 'How's your brother?' 'Good.' 'How's your sister?' 'Good.' That sort of thing. Then it was time to leave.

'Anh, what's your phone number?'

I gave him a dodgy one. It was strange to give my father a fake phone number but I didn't want him calling our house, just in case Mum or one of the kids picked up.

Then I drove all the way back to Sydney. It was a very long drive. I was emotionally spent. I was running on adrenalin, it was just too much—too many feelings, too many thoughts, too much confusion. I got home and fell onto my bed exhausted. I hadn't slept for twenty-six hours.

I didn't tell anyone about my meeting with Dad, not even Suzie. For a week I lived with a lot of uncertainty and questions mulling around in my head. Dad had acted like I'd gone away for a short holiday and recently come back. What I had really wanted from him was an apology, so I called him again.

This time he sounded different, his speech seemed affected by something. He was slurring severely. I hadn't noticed it so much when I'd seen him so I asked him what was wrong.

'Nothing wrong', he said quickly, too quickly. There was something going on but it was still too early for me to understand. Bloody hell. The guy sounded weird, so it was not really the time to launch into blame and anger, so I let it slide. I was also frightened. I wanted to reconnect with the man I used to know, not deal with some strange illness. Dad was quick to get me off the phone and I was glad he was letting me off the hook.

'I ne-ad to go. Cawl meee ba-ack soon, Anh. In a few we-eeks.'

'Okay, bye.'

A month later I flew down to see him again, this time with

Suzie. We arrived around midday and I'd prepared Suzie; I'd told her about my half brother, the other woman and the state of my dad.

What I hadn't prepared her for was Dad's showmanship.

When the battered front door of the housing commission unit opened, Suzie and I laid our eyes on the biggest seafood feast we'd ever seen. Dad's plastic table was covered with a mouth-watering banquet—lobster, crabs, prawns, scallops—that just didn't fit in with the surroundings. Dad had always loved seafood. When he won at the races, or when a big cheque came in from a delivery of garments, we'd be off to the fish markets. In this case he must have borrowed the money or at least spent their entire week's budget on this one meal for his son and his son's fiancée.

'Suzie!' he cried out.

My dad grabbed her hand with both of his and shook it vigorously. Suzie told me later that she liked him instantly.

What surprised me was Dad's speech. He sounded completely normal. We all got stuck into this enormous feast, talking, laughing, my father telling Suzie stories about 'When Anh was a kid'.

'Anh tell you about the time he stitched his finger to the business shirt? *RRRRAAAAAARRRRR!* 'Daaaad! Muuuuum! Heeeelp!'.'

'Anh has bad asthma, I stay awake with Anh all night watching the soccer till he tired enough to go to sleep.'

'You ever lock your keys in the car; just go see Anh!'

I realised that, when he wasn't drunk, this guy was indeed the most wonderful dad in the world. Somehow, during the past eight years I had managed to block out all the good memories and focused solely on what he'd done wrong. I realised I still very much loved this laughing, beautiful, terribly flawed man.

After the meal a cab came and picked up Suzie to return her to the airport. She had to get back to a court case in Sydney the next day. I was going to stay a few more days with Dad.

My father dragged the top mattress off his queen-sized bed

ensemble out to the living room for me to sleep on. We sat at the plastic table and talked late into the night, and I realised that as Dad got tired, his speech started faltering again. Not as bad as it was on the phone, but enough for me to notice. There had been talk of an illness from Dad's partner at the first visit but it was glossed over, and now I really wanted to know. All the facts, everything.

I thought, *Just ask him what's going on.* But I didn't. I put it off. I was scared of what he might tell me. *Okay*, I decided, *I'll just have another glass of wine and then I'll ask him about his health.*

All of a sudden, he started wobbling in his chair and said, 'I'm just going to have a lie down.'

Dad awkwardly slid off the chair and slumped down on the mattress a metre away. I watched in horror as he curled up into a trembling ball and started crying.

Suzie and I had a long engagement because we wanted to save some money, and we were only twenty-two. I had a few thousand stashed away from casual work, and the comedy was starting to take off, so a couple of weeks after proposing to her we went shopping for what was going to be my biggest purchase ever.

One afternoon I went to Suzie's office at Allen, Allen & Hemsley, one of the biggest law firms in the country, to take her shopping. Suzie was wearing a beautiful business suit but I was dressed for a comedy performance I was booked for later that night. In my early years I used to do gigs in old jeans, a flannelette shirt and thongs. Not just any thongs, but Kmart double pluggers that had worn so thin I could tell you when I stepped on a coin whether it was heads or tails.

It dawned on me that when you go shopping for expensive jewellery you really shouldn't look like you're casing the joint. Everywhere we went people looked at us strangely, because it looked like Suzie was my lawyer, and we'd just gotten out of a trial where she had to defend me for an armed hold-up. I've never seen shop assistants so nervous. One section of a particular shop had two extra doors to get through and, as soon as we got past the second entry, there were three staff and a security guard hovering near us and watching me like a hawk.

'Maybe you'd prefer to look at these ones over here', the senior shop assistant said, shooing us over to the cheaper rings with diamonds the size of a grain of sand. 'They might be more in your price range.'

Being the proud young suitor that I was, I was offended.

'Actually, these diamonds are a little small. Got anything bigger?'

At this point I could tell the lady was thinking I was about to pull down a balaclava and Suzie was going to reveal that under her suit coat she was hiding a sawn-off shot gun. She scurried off and came back with the manager. He was a short Italian man desperately trying to look imposing and official. Then he saw me and his face lit up, 'Anh!'

A couple of weeks earlier I had been on a TV special and the owner had seen the show. He gave me a special discount—'Only for-a you. You-a da funny guy on-a da TV'—on a stunning diamond ring, which put me in the good books for a long, long time.

We decided to have a huge engagement party. In Vietnam, as soon as you got engaged you started calling your in-laws Mum and Dad, so it's a much bigger deal than in Aussie culture.

'Let's do a big traditional Vietnamese thing, the whole shebang', Suzie declared when I told her about its significance. I was over the moon.

'What do my parents have to do?' she asked.

'They don't have to do anything.'

'My mum is desperate to do something', she persisted.

'Okay. We'll bring most of the food but you provide some food as well.'

In Vietnam it's traditional for the groom's family to bring a barbecued pig to the engagement party. The size of the pig is meant to be a reflection of the wealth and resources you can bring to the children's marriage—so everyone goes all out, and we too wanted to make an impressive splash. The morning of the party, Mum, Tram and I went out and bought one of the biggest pigs we could find. It was over a metre long.

'Wait till they see this', Mum said, as our family made the drive from Yagoona to Suzie's house. The big grin was soon wiped off Mum's face when we reached Wahroonga, an old-money area full of huge blocks, long driveways, beautiful gardens and majestic houses in the northern suburbs of Sydney. The streets were littered with BMWs, Porsches and Maseratis. I had been here many times but for my mother and her brothers and sisters, this was way outside their comfort zone. My family was awestruck.

There were forty people from my extended family attending the party. We parked our Camrys, Datsuns and Daewoos on the road and waited on the edge of the property until the rest turned up. When they did we all huddled together and I phoned Suzie.

'You ready?'

'Yep, we're ready', she replied.

'Okay. Let's do it.'

The driveway was massive, about fifty metres long. We walked past the tennis court and onto a circular drive with manicured plants and a huge statue of a Roman goddess in the middle.

'I saw something like this in a movie once', one of my uncles said. As we reached the end of the driveway, my mother spotted a stone fountain and lost it.

'Why didn't you tell me how rich they are?'

'I told you they were wealthy. Five-bedroom house.'

'Do you think we need a bigger pig?' she whispered.

We turned the corner and Mum saw the swimming pool, and yet more fountains. It was just too much.

'Oh my god . . . this pig's nowhere near big enough!'

'Shush up. Just keep walking.'

We were in full view of Suzie's family by now. The pig, cooked and ready to eat, sat on a large wooden platter and was carried up the driveway by two grown men.

'Where's the closest pig shop?' Mum whispered loudly, giving away her panic. 'Let's go get a giant pig. Huge.' She turned to Uncle Khanh, her youngest brother, who owned a Toyota Celica, the fastest of all the family's cars.

'Khanh, can we go and get a bigger one? How far to shops?' The stress was pouring out of her.

'Mum, just calm down', I pleaded. By now, I was freakin' out too. Mum was consumed by the fear that Suzie's parents would think me and my family would not be rich enough to take care of their daughter in the manner they expected. She was becoming obsessed with the pig and she wasn't the only one. As men often do, I had forgotten to tell Suzie's family a few minor details about the party; among them, the fact that we would be bringing a metre-long pig with us.

Suzie's mother's eyes were popping out as she stared at this glazed, glistening carcass being carried up her driveway.

'Oh my god, Suzie, what on earth is that?'

Eventually we arrived at the house. As we entered the double front doors I caught sight of Suzie and momentarily lost my breath. She had secretly organised with my mother to wear a traditional Vietnamese dress. She was dazzling.

The two clans faced up to each other and there was a lot of awkward smiling and nodding. It was incredibly nerve-racking, partly because my mother didn't know Suzie's parents. She had only met them once, briefly, at an informal afternoon tea a few weeks earlier. We had become engaged so quickly after we started dating. My mum was hiding behind Uncle Dung and in her panic she'd forgotten that she was the one who must speak first. Uncle Dung's wife pushed Mum forward, and she stood there, stunned. The speech my sister had helped her prepare had escaped her mind and she stared blankly at the thirty pairs of eyes that were staring back at her. She decided to speak from the heart.

'My son lup your dotter berry much. Anh tek care of Suzie like he tek care of us. He will lup her like he lup his family. Anh has very big lup. When he lup someone he mek sure dey happy forever.'

I looked across at my gorgeous fiancée and Suzie's eyes were full of tears. Mum went on.

'Today I berry happy too, because today I have a new dotter. I promise you, all my family will lup Suzie and look after her. Tank you.'

The whole place broke out in applause. There were sniffles, handshakes and backslaps all round. The ice was broken instantly and two families came together united by our lup. It was wonderful.

When it was time to eat, my aunty asked Suzie's mother if our family could use her kitchen. With a quick nod from Frances, twenty Vietnamese women descended on the room. They opened up every cupboard, like police searching for drugs. They were looking for a meat cleaver but none was to be found.

'What kind of people don't have a meat cleaver?' my aunty muttered, then turned to me. 'Anh, ask them why they hide their meat cleaver in a secret place?'

All Asian households keep a large cleaver, like a butcher's. Aussies don't have them and my family wondered how they were going to chop up the freakin' giant hog.

'Can we use your knives?' my mother asked Suzie's mother. My mother-in-law stood there, amused and bemused, as all these Vietnamese women in colourful traditional dress turned into ninjas, weighing up whatever knives they could lay their hands on. None of them were big enough. Finally they found a large knife but it wouldn't cut through the skin. They scavenged around for any large, heavy objects to use as an anvil to force the knife through.

'Ah-ha', Aunty Huong shouted out. She'd found a frozen chicken. *Whack, whack, whack*. Nothing like the sound of frozen chook on knife on crackling to tell you you're in for a feast.

All my other aunties had gathered around to prepare the soup and seafood in a huge whirl of activity. It was like a scene from a movie: frantic, noisy pandemonium in the kitchen, cut to elegant lounge room with people having polite conversation, cut back to the kitchen and, presto, all the food lies beautifully presented and ready to eat. It was a proper Vietnamese banquet: pork, dumplings, spring rolls, you name it. Suzie's father joked afterwards, 'I have two sons and I want them to marry Vietnamese girls. I want more of this delicious pork!'

On the other side of the serving table, the Aussie side, stood an array of barbecued chickens, salads, lamingtons and even a pavlova with passionfruit and cream. It was a truly multicultural meal. Everyone started eating and got into the spirit of the day. The house looked like both our families had known each other for years. Uncle Thanh had half of Suzie's family gathered around him as he told them war stories.

'Shoot, run, the plane come down. *Bang!*' They were rapt.

Over on the other side of the room, my mother and aunts were giving Suzie's mother and family tips about where to buy the best silk in Sydney and admiring each other's clothes.

'Where'd you get that lovely fur jacket?' one of them asked Uncle Dung's wife.

'My husband buy for me . . . you like it? It's antique . . . very expensive.'

Luckily Uncle Dung had remembered to remove the fifty-cent price tag.

My family loved Suzie, and every time they knew she was coming over they would prepare a different delicacy for her. After around three-dozen such dishes, they were running out of ideas and started getting into the really exotic stuff. One night we turned up at a family get-together and uncle Dung was very excited.

'Suzie. I made special one for you. This one called Vietnamee Pizza!'

Oh my god, Uncle Dung, you didn't. I love Uncle Dung and most of the time his immaturity is charming, but sometimes you just want to strangle him. 'Vietnamese Pizza' is a nickname my family gave to a dish made up of duck's blood. The blood settles like jelly, and you sprinkle nuts and herbs and duck meat on top, hence giving it the appearance of a pizza. It's kind of like Scottish black pudding—slimy and soft with just a hint of that metallic taste you get when you accidentally bite your lip.

He lifted up the plate to show Suzie and she genuinely smiled, excited by this dish. I realised she had no idea what it was.

'You have to try it! You have to try it!'

Uncle Dung was joined by my aunties and little cousins, they descended on her like a pack of wolves hungry for a laugh—Anh's Aussie fiancée was about to try one of the yuckiest dishes in the culinary universe. My mum tried to save her.

'Suzie . . . you don't have to eat it. It's duck's blood.'

Suzie turned pale.

'You've got to be kidding. Is that really duck's blood?' she whispered to me. I nodded.

'Do I have to eat it?'

'Nah. They're just kidding around, they're teasing you.'

She straightened up.

'I'll eat it.'

My family giggled like five-year-olds as she put it in her mouth.

'It's delicious', she declared.

'Oh my god! Suzie ate it!' My aunties were howling with laughter. 'Even we don't eat that strange crap!'

Over the coming months Suzie endured wave after wave of

'strange crap': chicken embryos, pig intestines and ox tongue. She put it all down with a smile on her face.

'This girl's a champion!' my grandma declared. 'She's more Vietnamese than you lot!'

Family dinners at our place always get a little crazy. Uncle Huy, the priest with the large bottom, was at one time a resident chaplain in the Australian Army and he had been training regularly with his soldiers. Half way through dinner he asked me: 'What are you leg pressing at the moment?'

I usually leg press around a hundred and twenty kilograms, depending on whether I've been going to the gym or not.

'A hundred or thereabouts', I replied. 'What about you?'

'I'm doing a hundred and forty', he said.

This is the kind of situation where I play the good nephew. You see, I knew he was talking pounds, not kilograms. One hundred and forty pounds is only about sixty kilograms. I could have easily pointed this out and won the game, but I didn't because he's my uncle, and he is everyone's favourite priest because he does your standard metric one-hour mass in around thirty-five minutes. Many a hot Sunday morning he'd blessed the parish with a short sermon, a quick service and an early mark home. I owed him for this.

'A hundred and forty! Wow, that's fantastic!' I'd say.

A couple of Christmases ago, he got overly excited.

'Anh, you and me, see who's got the harder thighs. C'mon, World Championship Thigh-off!' It was Christmas and we were a little drunk, so we both got up and twenty-five or so members of our family started feeling the hardness of a priest and a comedian's quadriceps.

'Suzie, touch it!' my mum said to her, pointing to the two sets of thighs flexed while precariously balancing on the dining room chairs. It was up to Suzie to decide the winner.

'So who won?'

'Umm . . . Uncle Huy by far!' she declared. The whole family were hysterical.

I couldn't believe it so I reached across and flicked Uncle Huy's thigh. Solid as a rock. I had gritted my teeth, screwed up my eyes—and flexed as hard as I could, and got beat fair and square. I thought years and years of playing rugby league and training twice a week was going to get me across the line. I guess I forgot he had just as many years hiking up and down the mountainous jungles of Vietnam carrying a commando's rations on his back.

I faced my own trials when I went over to Suzie's house for a meal. Dinner at Suzie's was almost the exact opposite to ours, especially when it was a special occasion. It was like a fine restaurant; you sat down and conversed. You didn't shout, yelp, or flex any leg muscles, you conversed. In the beginning I kept looking into the corners of the room, half expecting a courteous yet quick-witted English butler to appear and gently lay a starched, monogrammed napkin on my thigh.

'Lovely to see you again, Mr Do, sir.'

On one early visit they planned a 'special dinner', and I knew it was special because Suzie's mum had pulled out her enormous box of silverware, polished it and laid it just so on the table. There must have been three or four forks, several knives of different sizes and a single spoon to every setting.

As we sat down I started sweating. I had not been to many formal dinners and I had no idea which piece of cutlery to use. Where was the chopstick option? I have since been told you start from the outside and work your way in but, on this occasion, I had not heard this titbit of wisdom.

A number of entrees came out and I was doing pretty well, I thought. I soon figured out I should eat slowly, watch to see what everyone else was using and follow suit. A main dish came out and I was watching Suzie's grandmother, who picked up her spoon. No problem. I picked up the spoon and began happily scooping up the peas and little veggies on the plate. Made perfect sense. I looked up and I realised her grandma was just re-arranging her cutlery to make space for a carafe of red wine. She put the spoon back on the table, and picked up a fork. *She bloody tricked me!*

We got to the end of the night and out came dessert—a special custard dish. A very, very runny special custard dish. Everyone picked up their spoon and I looked down. All I had left was a fork. I looked at Suzie's grandmother who looked at my fork. *I know I have a fork, you know I have a fork, everyone knows Anh's got a freakin' fork.*

But no one said anything and I finished off my dessert, taking a little longer than everyone else. To this day Suzie's dad likes to remind me of the event. He'll sling me a steak at a barbie and say, 'Hang on, Anh, let me get you a spoon for that.'

On another occasion I came over one afternoon and saw Suzie's dad jackhammering old tiles off his pool so that workers could put in new pebblecrete. I had never used a jackhammer before, but I figured it couldn't be that hard, so I said to him, 'Robert, why don't you take a break. I'll do a bit for you.'

He showed me how it worked and then handed me the jack-hammer. *Bam bam bam bam bam* . . . away I went. Half an hour later I wondered, *Is this guy coming back from his break? I'll just keep going I suppose.* Two hours later I was still going at it. Suzie called out: 'Anh, take a break.'

I took a three-minute drink break then got stuck into it again. I figured I'd better just keep going until Robert came out and told me to stop. *Bam bam bam bam bam* . . . another three hours later I'd finished the entire pool.

I walked in to dinner with my teeth rattling and my fingers trembling from the vibration the jackhammer had set into my bones. I picked up my knife . . . *tap tap tap tap tap* on the plate.

Suzie told me later that Robert was inside the whole time watching me.

'I can't believe he's still going', he'd said. 'I just want to see how much resilience the kid's got.'

'Trust me, Dad, I know Anh. He can keep going till tomorrow morning if need be.'

After I'd finished the whole pool Robert said to his wife: 'Fantastic! I liked this kid from the start.'

And indeed he had. Years ago when Suzie and I were just friends he said to her, 'You'll marry that boy one day'. He saw in me a young kid who reminded him of himself. Robert had also been raised by a single mother and had grown up in a suburb not far from Yagoona.

Our wedding reception was to be held at Taronga Zoo and it was going to be expensive. Suzie's father wouldn't let our family pay, especially after all the trouble we had gone to with the engagement party.

'In Australia, the bride's family pays. That's how we do things', he told me.

'In Vietnam we split it and all pitch in together', I countered. He waved me away.

'No, Anh, it's different here, so I'll take care of it.'

'How about we go halves', I said, thinking I'd do the right thing and make one last offer to be sure I looked like a good bloke, and then I'd let it go.

'All right', he said.

All right? Oh my god, the guy just said 'All right'. Anh, you idiot! I went into panic mode as large dollar figures popped into my mind, a swarm of zeros swirling around like poisonous killer bees. *Quick, say something to try and reverse the 'All right'.*

'All right, Anh, I'll tell you what, why don't you take care of the alcohol and the entertainment?'

Phew! I was happy with that. I really didn't want him to take care of all of it, but I was glad that our going halves deal meant he had by far the biggest half.

Over the years Robert has become a friend and somewhat of a mentor to me, teaching me the strategies he used to become very successful financially. But in the early days I was trying extremely hard just to impress him. I knew he liked wines and he would probably want really fancy ones at the wedding, so I came up with a genius plan.

'Robert, Frances, next week I am going to bring over six reds and six whites and I want you to do a blind tasting.'

I shopped all around Sydney comparing prices and found a dozen fantastic wines, which were all on special. They ranged from a thirty-dollar red down to a six-dollar white. I got Suzie's parents to sit down in the living room, and then the two of us treated them to this brilliant tasting, complete with cheese and crackers in between glasses to 'cleanse the palate'.

First I poured out the most expensive riesling, hoping the initial sip would be slightly jarring, and put him off.

'Oh that's delicious!' he said.

Damn! He liked it. Let's just hope he likes the others more.

When I poured the last white, the six-dollar chardonnay that was reduced from $28, Robert and Frances took a sip and both agreed in unison: 'This one's the best.'

Whoo-hoo! I was over the moon. It really was a good wine, and when you multiply the saving of $22 per bottle over multiple cases, it tasted even better. Alas, they went on to pick a red that was $25 a bottle. But what the heck, one bargain out of two ain't bad, and it certainly could've been much, much worse. More importantly, Robert and Frances liked this quirky young kid who was so very keen to impress their family. And so the stage was set for a wedding to remember, with just one little wonky-toothed issue which remained unsolved.

The wedding was held in my old school chapel at St Aloysius College in Kirribilli. It was a Catholic ceremony and about a hundred and fifty guests turned up to watch us take our vows. The service was led by my muscle-thighed Jesuit priest uncle, as well as my favourite priest from school, Father Dooley. It was a beautiful sunny day with a few clouds overhead and everything was going perfectly, just like a fairytale, until something unexpected tripped me up.

It had been a little while since I had attended a Vietnamese wedding, so I had forgotten about a traditional song dedicated to the happy couple's parents. One of my distant cousins picked up a guitar and dedicated the song to the bride and groom's mums and dads. *No sweat*, I thought. *This should be good.* And then the lyrics started.

Dear Lord, watch over my father and mother . . .

I was thinking, *Sweet. Lovely song isn't it?*

For me the mountains you've climbed,
The struggles you've gladly endured . . .

Uh oh, I thought to myself.

No matter what happens tomorrow
Your love I shall never forget
Your love I shall always return . . .

I felt a lump in my throat, but clenched my teeth and managed to swallow it back . . . just. Then I did something stupid, I looked down at my mum. She saw me trying to hold it back, and she started crying. That's when I completely lost it. I was bawling. I looked down and saw my loving, beautiful mother who had sacrificed so much to get me to where I was. I saw my little sister and brother, two little kids who had endured it all. And I thought about my dad who wasn't there. Who would've given the world to see his son not waste any time, and marry the woman he loves.

My dad had known about the wedding, we had talked about it a few months earlier.

'Look, Anh, it'll be weird if everyone sees me, so it's probably best if I'm not there', he said, wanting to get in first. He knew I wasn't going to invite him, and I loved him for making it easier for me.

I looked across at my beautiful bride, my soul mate, my best friend and lover who just radiated a warmth that told me everything was going to be okay. Suzie wiped away my tears and I thanked God for my blessed life.

I expected to get a severe ribbing from my football mates after the ceremony for my show of emotion, but instead the boofheads hugged me. Big Sid, normally a stoic Italian, came up to me still teary eyed and crushed me with a big hairy hug.

'Ya dickhead', he said. *Sniff, sniff.*

Our friends told us later that as we had said 'I do' the sun broke through the clouds and a blaze of light shone through the massive stained-glass window at the front of the chapel. It was a magical omen. Suzie did a reading in Vietnamese and my family just loved it; she had made such an effort to embrace our culture.

The ceremony was emotional and moving but the reception was one enormous party. Suzie always loves to do things a bit differently so ours was never going to be a conventional wedding. We had our traditional church ceremony, but the theme for the reception was Caribbean Carnivale. It was awesome. There were multi-coloured flowers, butterflies and bridesmaid dresses—bright colours everywhere.

I had approached a friend from the stand-up circuit who ran a theatre props hire business.

'How much you got, Anh?'

'Three thousand.'

For that, Suzie and I chose quite a few decorations but on the wedding day he surprised us. He emptied his entire showroom into this function centre and decked it out with decorations worth five times what we had paid him. When the guests turned up they saw a rickshaw out the front and palm trees and toucans around the entrance. Peacocks from the zoo joined in and strutted around as well. Dad would have loved the birds. Inside, the centre resembled a tropical jungle. There were crazy circus mirrors and a huge butterfly above the bridal table. It looked fantastic.

We had hired a four-piece band but we also had a musical surprise. One week before the wedding I was walking down the street and saw a pan-pipe group from Chile.

'What are you guys doing next Saturday?' I asked. They were available, and we agreed on a price. When the guests turned up at Taronga Zoo, they were greeted by the sounds of the Andes as they entered the jungle within.

The highlight of the speeches was my mother's, translated from Vietnamese by my brother.

'I am looking forward to looking after some babies', she said, looking at Suzie. 'If you don't have any, I will.'

There was lots of laughter from both sides of the family, and I was especially glad she hadn't told her favourite 'Anh story' which dated back to when I was a baby.

In Vietnam, it was easier to breastfeed babies than wean them. In my case, I was breastfed until I was three. Mum tells the story of how when Khoa was only six months old, he had to compete with me for breast milk. Whenever I did something good, Mum would say, 'That's because I breastfed him until three'.

Good marks at school? 'Breastfed until three. It's good for the brain.'

Did well on *Dancing with the Stars*. 'Breastfed until three.'

Won a comedy competition. 'That's 'cos I breastfed him till he was three!'

Years later, when Suzie and I had our own child, she asked Mum how long she should breastfeed.

'Oh, only a year, it's a pain in the arse.'

Suzie and I had our dramatic departure from the wedding prepared— a water taxi was waiting for us down at the zoo's wharf, but how to get there? When I'd hired the prop rickshaw from my mate I'd asked him if it was operational.

'Nah, it's just for show.' he said. 'You can sit on it for photos, but don't try to ride it.'

On the night as we waved goodbye to the large crowd gathered outside the function room Suzie and I looked at our rickshaw.

'What do you reckon?' I said.

She gave me one of her light-up-the-room smiles and said, 'What the hell, let's go out with a bang!'

I got in the driver's seat and Suzie jumped into the bucket chair. With a bride in the back, a bottle of red wine in the belly, and a deluded confidence, I took off in the just-for-show rickshaw. As soon as I started pedalling I realised why this was a stupid idea, but it was too late.

The road from the zoo entrance down to the wharf is one of the steepest declines in all of Sydney. Once we took off, there was no stopping us. Suzie screamed loudly as we picked up ridiculous speed.

'Slow down!' she yelled.

'I can't!' I had tested the brakes earlier on flat ground and they seemed fine. I didn't factor in an extra fifty-kilograms of wife and a curving, forty-five degree downhill run. All I could hear was: '*AAAAAAHHHHHHHHHHHH!!!!!*'

And that was just me.

Suzie was screaming a bunch of things I couldn't hear, but I did make out single words every now and then: 'Stop! . . . Fall! . . . Die! . . . Kill You! . . . Divorce! . . . *AHHHHH!*'

Somehow we made it to the bottom alive and Suzie rushed out of the bucket seat, ran up to me, and gave me an enormous hug.

'You are an absolute nutter, Anh Do. But I love you!'

The next morning we two newlyweds flew off to Thailand for two weeks, on our honeymoon, not realising our lives were about to change in a way we'd never ever expected.

After our honeymoon we moved into an apartment in North Sydney. Suzie continued working as a lawyer and I was doing stand-up. I was offered the chance to do three shows in Melbourne and said 'Yep' straight away because I knew it would be a chance to hang out with my father.

When I do comedy, I have a huge props case where I keep all these funny things that I make jokes about in my stand-up routine. It's the size of a large suitcase. In Melbourne Dad would drive me to gigs. As soon as we stopped the car he would hop out and run round to the boot to grab the case before I could.

'Dad, it's heavy, let me carry it.'

'No, no, you're the main event tonight. I'm your roadie.' He'd walk off making himself laugh by going, 'Check-one-two. Check. Check. One. Two', like a guy testing a microphone. No matter how much I argued, he resisted. He was adamant that he was going to be my *dan em*.

My father grew up with many *dan ems*—young men who followed him around and did things for him because he was a natural leader. His nickname among his mates was 'Lee' which means judgement, and these young men trusted his judgement in a time of war. I dare say he'd probably never been a *dan em* himself before, and here he was volunteering, no, insisting, he was going to be one for his own son. It reminded me of occasions in my childhood when some Vietnamese men refused to call me Anh, and Dad wouldn't let it go until they did.

'It's his name. Call him by his proper name.'

Anh in Vietnamese means 'elder brother', and it's a title reserved for someone senior to yourself. So by giving his son the name, Dad made the world call me 'elder brother', and he made his little boy the chief.

I introduced Dad to my friend Dave Grant and Dave, ever the charmer, asked, 'So who is this Anh, your handsome brother?' Dad laughed loudly.

'No! I am his father!'

Dave became Dad's favourite comedian, after me of course.

I did a fantastic gig, and Dad was thrilled. We chattered away on the trip home, both of us on an adrenaline high. When we got back to his place we sat back to talk over a few beers. That was the night when he finally admitted to me that he had a tumour in his head. It was pressing against nerves in his brain, which caused him to slur his speech occasionally. He explained that he had good days and bad days, and that it was unpredictable and sporadic.

'What treatment are you on?' I asked him.

'I'll be okay', he said.

'What do you mean you'll be okay? You getting treatment?'

It turned out the idiot hadn't even started seeing a doctor until a few weeks beforehand. My dad likes taking care of things himself, and hates asking for help. Geez! I just don't understand . . .

People . . .

Like . . .

That . . .

God, we turn into our parents don't we? I finally saw the absurdity of my stubborn unwillingness to ask for assistance at school, getting into so much trouble for 'forgetting' my textbooks, for 'losing' my sports uniform, when I could have just told them the truth—'My mum can't afford the textbooks'—and the school would've sorted something out.

Dad took a huge gulp of beer.

'When the Lord wants me, he can take me. He can take this outlaw back', he said, staring off into the middle distance. 'And he may well punish me.'

It wasn't the earnest, heartfelt apology I was looking for, but it was an admission of sorts, and it was good enough for me. I remember when I was young, I never once heard my dad apologise to my mum directly, but he'd do this thing where he'd refer to himself in a less-than-glamorous, third-person kind of way.

'Well, this forgetful bastard made a mistake, didn't he?'

'Mum told me about the kid on the boat', I said. Dad took a deep breath and screwed up his eyes.

'That was an impossible situation', I assured him.

'I will never know, Anh. I will just . . . never . . . know.' He paused contemplatively. 'But what I know is this: I promised his mother I would deliver him safely.'

My mum, uncles and aunties all swear there was no way my father could've saved Loc when the seventeen-year-old kid jumped into the ocean. Dad had tied a rope around himself and ordered two of the men to hold onto it while he jumped in to search. Everyone on the boat pleaded with him not to jump—if Dad died, the trip was as good as over for everyone. That split-second decision not to go in haunted him forever.

'You always have to make decisions in your life, Anh. And don't kid yourself; when you don't decide, that's a decision.'

We sat in stillness for a while, staring at empty cans of beer and two empty bottles of wine. Then Dad began tapping his finger on the table repeatedly and looked down. I knew this was a sign he was about to say something out of character. Something he found hard to express.

'Anh, I didn't want to bring this up yet, but if I ever have to go anywhere, like . . . go . . . you know . . . for a long, long time—not that I'm intending to, but if it happens—there's just one thing I want to do first. I'd like to see your brother and your sister again. So I can tell them I love them. So they have no doubt that I love them.'

When I got back to Sydney I told Khoa I'd seen Dad and explained everything that'd happened.

'You should go and see him too, Khoa.'

'I don't want to.'

'No, man, you don't understand. There might not be much time left. You gotta go and see him.'

'No. Piss off!'

He walked into his room and slammed the door. I hadn't expected this reaction from him at all. How naive I was to forget the absolute fury I'd felt towards Dad the first time I went down to see him. I didn't say anything to Tram as I thought I'd have to figure out what to do with Khoa first—one at a time.

When I next saw Dad I told him it was going to take a little longer than I thought for them to come around.

'So how about this, Dad. You can't go anywhere until I get them to come round and see you?'

'Ahhh. Sure.' He looked up to the sky and announced: 'Sorry up there, you'll just have to wait, because this bastard's not going anywhere.' Then he smiled his wonky overconfident smile.

Every morning Suzie walked across the Harbour Bridge to work—a lovely way to start the day—then got bogged down in contracts, mergers and hostile takeovers—not so lovely. I knew she wasn't enjoying being a lawyer, from time to time she even talked about quitting and pursuing her creative interests, but she was reluctant to take the leap.

When I had been in Melbourne, Dad had asked me, 'Is Suzie happy, Anh?'

'Yeah, I think so. Why?'

'Make sure she's happy. Don't make the mistake I made. I took your mother for granted.'

One night I started to talk to Suzie about her work again.

'Are you happy being a lawyer, sweetheart?'

'Not really.'

'So why don't you quit?'

'I don't know, it's not that easy. It's a lot of money to walk away from.'

'Don't worry about the money, we'll manage. What matters is that you're happy.'

Unlike me, my wife is not one to make snap decisions, whether it's about her career or which placemats to buy at Ikea. She had to think about it for a while. In the end she quit, and there we were, a bunch of degrees and not a lawyer in sight. Suzie decided to go back and study writing and photography, which she enjoyed immensely.

We decided to move back to the house I'd bought for Mum in Yagoona for a short time while we looked for somewhere else to rent. It was a fantastic house, and I enjoyed working on the place, improving little bits and pieces that needed to be done. After all, I had been building birdcages, duck enclosures and golden pheasant pens since the age of twelve. However, there was a busted side gate that I had hastily repaired, and never got around to fixing properly.

One afternoon a huge storm came along and blew the bottom of the gate out.

Mum had owned two pug dogs called Nugget and Peanut for several years and now the little tackers decided to go exploring in the rain. We drove around for hours and hours trying to find them.

'Where are they going to sleep?' my mother whimpered. She usually cried only when she was happy, not when she was sad. But Mum wept openly about those two dogs. They were like extra children to her.

'Mum, go to sleep, it's all right', I said, trying to pacify her. 'I'm sure we'll find them tomorrow.' I was comforting myself as much as her.

The next day we made posters on the bus-crash computer, and went to the corner shop.

'Can I put these up on the wall?' The shop owner nodded.

'Hang on', he said. 'There was an old lady who came in yesterday and she told me she'd found a couple of dogs and needed to buy dog food. She lives just four doors down.' My eyes brightened.

'Did she say what type?'

'No, but she definitely said she was feeding two dogs.'

I bounded up to her front door and knocked vigorously. A small Asian woman appeared.

'Hello. The shop owner told me you found two dogs?'

'Yes, two dogs', she said, then turned around and started talking to Mum's dogs in Vietnamese.

'You're Vietnamese?' I said, in Vietnamese.

'And so are you', she replied, in Vietnamese. 'I knew these dogs belonged to Vietnamese people', she said. 'They speak Vietnamese.'

Ra day, ngoi soung, she said to the dogs, and they sat down as asked.

'I tried to feed them dog food but they preferred the pork soup I cooked for my grandson. They eat Vietnamese as well.'

'Thank you', I told her, and pressed some money into her hand. She didn't want it.

'Take it, please', I urged her. 'We were going to give it away as a reward anyway.'

With dogs in tow, I raced home. Mum was over the moon.

'This is best day of my life', she beamed. I kept thinking back to the day I bought her the house, but said nothing. As I left she was hugging her little Vietnamese speaking pugs like they were long-lost babies.

I just love animals. I'm sure it's a trait I got from my dad. Like him, I also have a habit of getting all excited about an idea, and going way over the top. When I started breeding fish, the house filled up quickly with twenty fish tanks. Then one day I was struck with bird fever.

It started at a Christmas party where someone gave Suzie's cousin a pair of lovebirds. I thought they were beautiful so, just like my dad would have done, the next day I went out and bought myself a crimson rosella, two lorikeets, five finches, and a corella. The corella was hand-reared and completely tame, in fact he thought he was a human being. I called him Pacino and taught him to say *Phoo Wah* like in *Scent of a Woman*. I even made a stand for him so he could have meals with us. He had his own little plate, and his own assigned seat at our dinner table.

Later on I bought a budgie as well. He was a cute little white thing and Suzie was quite attached to him. She named him Rocky. He and Pacino were good friends, but Pacino was my favourite. I trained him to poo on command. I would hold him over a litter tray and say, 'Poo!' And plop, out it would come. I taught him to do it on command in English and Vietnamese. I think he was Australia's only bilingual toilet-trained corella.

Unfortunately, I was starting to travel for comedy gigs and was away a week at a time. Pacino missed me. He had attached himself to me and, when I wasn't there, he would just squawk and squawk and *Phoo Wah* and squawk all day long. It would start at five in the morning and go till night.

It turned out he just didn't like women. Whenever Suzie went anywhere near him he would try to nip her. She thought it was just her, but then he began nipping at my mum as well. Up until now Suzie had been pretty relaxed about the aviary in our lounge room, but this behaviour tipped her over the edge.

'Pacino's a misogynist. A male chauvinist pig . . . bird. He has to go', she said.

What an ultimatum. The parrot or your wife.

I called up an old Vietnamese family friend who had been keen on the bird since I'd bought it.

'You know my bird, the one you're always talking about? I gotta find a new home for him. Do you want him?'

'Be over in ten minutes.'

He got to our place in five and took Pacino away. Suzie did a celebratory dance around the lounge room.

'Oh yeah . . . he's gone! *Phoo Wah* . . . he's gone!'

Two hours later, Suzie was printing photos in her darkroom with the door shut, so I knocked and called out, 'Guess what, sweetheart? Pacino's back.'

'Ha ha, very funny.' And then she heard him.

'*Phoo Wah*. SQUUAAAAWWWK! *Phoo Waaaah*.'

'You have got to be kidding! What bird did I torture in a past life to deserve this?'

The old man had a little Pomeranian dog, which hated the corella even more than Suzie. The two went at each other for two hours straight, so Pacino was sent packing. This time, though, Suzie was firm.

'He's not staying in this house!'

'Please! He loves me.'

'So does Phil, but you don't see him living in our lounge room, soiling himself every time he hears the word 'Poo'.'

On cue, Pacino dropped a greeny-grey splash onto the carpet.

I knew I'd lost, and so I said, 'Okay. He's gone.'

This time I called up the local pet shop, who asked me to bring him in.

'Please just find him a good home', I said.

'Does he talk? Any words at all?' the owner asked.

'Of course!'

Pacino belted out a bunch of hellos and 'want a scratch?' And, of course, *Phoo Wah*. For good measure he threw in *An com di* and *May im lung*—Vietnamese for 'Eat your dinner' and 'Shut the hell up!'.

'He speaks a bit of Vietnamese as well', I explained. But I had something even better to show him. 'Check this out . . . Poo!' And Pacino did.

The shop owner was beside himself.

'I've never seen that before! I'm going to keep this one for the shop—as a tourist attraction!'

• Ten •

Life was good. I was travelling around Australia doing stand-up and TV spots and as Suzie wasn't working so she came with me; it was like we were being paid to go on one big long holiday, except Anh had to go on stage and be funny for an hour or so every night. We had a wonderful time and met the friendliest people from all corners of Australia, from big cities to little country towns. Which is why the couple of times we ran into trouble really surprised us.

At one club a typical bouncer stood at the door, sporting a white shirt and black bowtie. I started filling in the temporary membership form everyone has to complete when they entered a club. The security guy drawled, slow and flat, 'No, mate, we don't really like your types in here'.

'No worries, mate, I'm the comedian. I'm just working', I replied.

'Very funny, mate.' He didn't believe me and stepped right up close to my face to make his point. 'Piss off.'

Even though the guy was a metre wide with a neck the size of a tree trunk, a younger, angrier, teenage Anh might've taken a swing at him just for the principle of it. But the past year, having found my dad and got married, had mellowed me. I was still annoyed though.

'Mate', I said, 'you go in and tell the manager that Anh Do, the comedian, is here. Tell him to come out and get me. And if he doesn't come out in five minutes, I'm going home. But you'll still have to pay me, mate, because it's in the contract. So go get him now, or you won't have a comedian.'

He turned around slowly and dawdled over to the manager, who came back, looked me up and down and took me in. There was no apology or admission of a mix up.

I did the show and everything was fine. On the way out, though, Suzie wanted to have a word about the issue with someone in charge. I told her not to worry about it—it wasn't worth it. But Suzie was incensed. Being blonde and blue eyed, she'd never really experienced this sort of overt racism before. I guess I was more used to it, even though it was a very rare occurrence. When my friend Dave advised me as a young comedian to take on all gigs, and not shy away from the hard ones, I took it on board. I was a specialist with the toughest, roughest crowds around—bikies, drunken yobbos and the like—I sometimes got heckled racially even before I got to the microphone. For me it was all part of the training. Suzie, on the other hand, was shocked and outraged.

'Go on, Anh, deck him.'

'Honey, he's enormous.'

'I've seen you belt bigger guys than him in footy games.'

'Thanks, sweetheart, but look, we've got the cash. Let's just go and have a nice dinner.'

'Well he's lucky, because you would've smashed him.' And she pecked me on the cheek.

In truth the guy would've left my head looking like Vietnamese Pizza, but I loved my wife for making me feel like I could've beaten the guy if I'd chosen to. Suzie understands me better than anyone else in the world. She knew the bouncer's opinions didn't matter to me one bit, but what *she* thought about me meant everything. She had just given me the opportunity to 'let the prick off'.

Not long after that incident I encountered the hardest gig of my life. There are certain comedy shows a Vietnamese comic should just flat out never be booked for. Ever.

I was on the wings waiting to go on stage. There were about two hundred old drunk guys in the crowd. *No problem.* Old drunk guys are a fantastic audience, they laugh at just about anything. *This is going to be easy.* Then the MC got going.

'Ahem, welcome to tonight's show everyone. But tonight, before we start, I'd like to ask everyone to bow their heads and observe a minute's silence for all our fallen brothers in World War Two, Korea, and Vietnam.'

Bloody hell! Who organised this gig?

So there were two hundred guys sitting quietly remembering fallen comrades who were shot by Asian men, and I'm waiting to go on to do thirty minutes of funny stuff. The MC concluded the minute's silence and continued.

'Okay, everyone, we're going to cheer up now and have a laugh. Please welcome our comedian . . .' He looked down at the piece of paper he was holding and looked at my funny, difficult-to-pronounce name. He squinted at it, then turned to the side of the stage and saw me.

'Jesus Christ!' he said out loud.

He was just as shocked as I was. He then looked up and said with a perfectly straight face, 'Please put your hands together for our comedian . . . Duncan O'Reilly.'

He hobbled off and had a chuckle to himself. Two hundred old guys started applauding . . . until they saw me walk out.

Funny looking O'Reilly! They must have been thinking. The applause quickly died away.

I looked out and the tension in the air was so thick, you could cut it with a knife. Someone at the back coughed, then we were back to a deafening silence. I broke the silence with my first joke, my opener, a killer . . . nothing. Second joke . . . still nothing. I did a full five minutes to complete silence, except for one noise. A gentleman sitting on a table to my right had one of those red bulbous golf ball noses that some old men get, which was made even redder by the dozen or so beers he'd had. He held out his right middle and index fingers in the shape of a gun, and he shot imaginary bullets at me.

Pap!

Pap!

Pap pap pap!

I tried to ignore him, just moved on to my next joke as quickly as possible.

Pap pap pap!…Pap!

I couldn't pretend I hadn't noticed, and so I said with a nervous smile, 'Sir, you've probably killed a few guys who look like me'.

Everyone looked on, waiting for his response. It was one word.

'Fourteen.'

He'd killed fourteen Vietnamese in the war.

What do I do now? To be fair just before I went on stage the club events guy realised how absurd the situation was and said to me, 'Mate, we've got the wrong comedian for the wrong night. Not your fault so just do five minutes. If it's not going well, just hop off, we'll still pay you the cash.'

Quitting seemed a very attractive option at this point in time, but do I just walk off and call it a night before things get worse, or should I try one last thing? Dave used to say the hard gigs were an opportunity to test your mettle: 'Learn from them Anh, treat them like a rare gift'.

I decided to bring forward all the material that would prove to them I was just an Aussie kid. So I did a number of jokes about bull terriers and Datsuns and housing commission estates, and slowly I was getting a few chuckles. Then I moved on to footy jokes, farming jokes and kiwi jokes. Slowly, slowly, I won them over. The old guys finally realised that if they closed their eyes, this Vietnamese kid was actually just an Aussie comedian up there talking about his working-class childhood.

It wasn't the best gig of my life, but it was one of the greatest experiences of my career. After the show an old guy came up to me, slapped me on the back and said, 'Geez, you're funny for a slope'. I could tell from his demeanour that he meant it as a compliment, so I took it as one.

'I'll buy you a beer, son', he added. So there I was having a drink with this guy, Paul, and three other guys came over and joined us. They started telling me war stories about their Vietnamese soldier mates, people like my uncles. It was wonderful to hear my dad and uncles' stories confirmed by Aussie diggers.

I told them that one of my uncles was kind of like a sapper, he'd done some clearing of landmines during the war.

'Anh!' Paul piped up excitedly. 'The first line of Jimmy Barnes' song 'Khe Sanh' is 'I left my heart to the sapper's round Khe Sanh'.'

What an amazing realisation. All these years, Barnesy had been singing about my uncle and I didn't even know because no one could understand Barnesy!

Then Eric, the funniest of the old guys, said, 'Isn't that interesting, Anh, that one of Australia's favourite songs is about a little Vietnamese town called Khe Sanh. If you ever want to be a rock star, go back to Vietnam and bring out a song called 'Albury Wodonga'!'

For me one of the greatest charms of doing stand-up around Australia is meeting the characters. I sat and drank and laughed with these four guys for several hours. Eric then said something else that stuck with me.

'You know why we lost the war, Anh? It was all those bloody tunnels that the communists dug. We could never do that. You know why? Because with us Aussies, for every one guy who's digging there's got to be five standing around having a smoko.' We all threw back our heads and roared.

A couple of nights later I did a show with Dave and I told him all about it. He slapped me hard on the back and said, 'Congratulations! Anh, you will never ever do a gig harder than that in your life. Consider that from now on, you shall have no fear of an audience because they'll all be easy compared to those old soldiers.'

He was right. That gig was the greatest gift, because I have not since encountered an audience even remotely that terrifying.

I was starting to do a lot more TV work now, making appearances on bigger programs like *The Footy Show* and *Rove*. Many of these were filmed in Melbourne and if they were Dad would always pick me up from the airport. At the time he had a couple of the crappiest cars you ever saw. One was a van and its engine was so loud that we simply couldn't speak to each other while he was driving. It was like trying to talk over the sewing machines when we were kids. At the traffic lights, he'd stop and I'd try to get a quick question in.

'So how you been, Dad?' He'd start to answer me and then the lights would change, *RRRAAAARRRRR!* the deafening noise would start again. It was the only time in my life when I was grateful for bad traffic. Our staccato conversations would last the whole distance from the airport to his place.

Dad drove me to a TV appearance on the talk show *Rove Live*. We arrived at the front gates and the security guard must've freaked out about the Sherman tank he'd heard approaching. The guy took one look at our van and pointed us over to where the audience parked their cars.

'Thank you', Dad said, and he started to head over there. Then the guard looked into the passenger side.

'One second, sir.' He squinted at me. 'You're Anh Do! Oh, I do apologise, you're on the show tonight.' He pointed us over to the VIP parking.

Dad drove his tank over and parked behind a row of black limousines. On the show that night were a bunch of superstars, including the American actor, Will Smith. Dad patted me on the shoulder.

'How good's this, Anh?' We both laughed and laughed, realising the ridiculousness of the situation. Dad then grabbed my props case like the devoted roadie he was and we marched on in to film my live TV spot, which went magnificently well.

As I headed back to my dressing room a huge big guy in sunglasses stopped me in the hallway. He was one of Will Smith's large entourage and he said in a rapper voice so deep it sounded like Barry White's uncle, 'I don't really know what you were talking about, but they seemed to love it'.

My own entourage, which consisted of one skinny Vietnamese man with his pullover tucked deep into his pants and wearing the biggest grin I've ever seen, put out his hand and shook the big guy's hand.

'This is my son', Dad said proudly.

We went back to Dad's place and cracked open some wine. When Dad was in a heightened state of happiness he liked to reminisce about old times. The happier he was, the further back he'd go. On this particular night, after seeing his son share the spotlight with Will Smith, Dad began talking about his eldest brother. Even in a drunken fog, my ears pricked up. Mum had told me that Uncle One had been murdered, but she'd never told me how. In fact, no one in the family ever dared talk about *how*. Except for Dad. And now Dad was about to tell me.

Uncle One's name was Binh. He was the eldest of the ten children, and according to family folklore he was the most kind and gentle person. With their father often away at war, Uncle One took it upon himself to help his mother raise his nine younger siblings. He was the apple of my grandmother's eye and had entered a seminary to study to become a priest. Everyone loved him.

When my family were planning to leave Vietnam, they pooled all their money together until they had enough to buy a boat. Uncle One was the eldest and Dad the most brash. The two of them negotiated to buy a boat on the black market and then travelled south for many, many hours to arrive at the bay where they were to meet the sellers.

When they came face-to-face with three men, they were told that only one person was to come with them to inspect the boat, which was moored another half hour's trek away. If there were more people, the communist guards would become suspicious. Dad volunteered to go, but Uncle One insisted that Dad should stay and wait, and that he'd go. So Dad and Uncle One split up the boat money between the two of them, and Uncle One went with the men, while Dad waited. An hour later . . . no Uncle One. An hour and a half later . . . no Uncle One.

'I had an ill feeling in my stomach, Anh, like something was wrong.' Dad looked up to the ceiling, and his face turned a deep red. 'I felt an urge to go down the track, to see what had happened . . . in fact, as soon as Uncle One left with them, I felt an urge to track behind them.'

I listened stunned.

'I didn't follow. I just waited.'

'That's what you were supposed to do, Dad.'

'No . . . no, I was supposed to follow them when I felt the urge. But I didn't.' He was holding back tears. 'I didn't because . . . I was scared.' Now he was crying.

'Did you go in later?' I asked him.

'No. I turned around and went all the way back home . . . without my brother . . . because I was scared.'

I'd never seen my father this honest before in my life. He took a huge gulp of beer, spilling it all over his mouth; it mixed with his tears and ran down his shirt.

'The next day I returned with some of your uncles . . . we went into the village and asked around. An old lady told us that her neighbours had seen something strange in the bamboo bushes. We went in and found Uncle Binh's body.'

As Dad said these words he broke down completely. He pounded on his chest in rage and sadness, sobbing violently, and said to himself: 'I'm sorry, Mother. I'm so sorry, Mother. I'm sorry for brother Binh's death, Mother.'

In that moment I fully understood my father's life philosophy: There's only two times in life, there's now and there's too late.

The next morning Dad was driving me back to the airport so I could return to Sydney. 'So . . . how's your health, Dad?' It was the standard answer I got.

'Look at me . . . a hundred per cent', followed by a grin.

'You still seeing a doctor?'

'Of course I am.'

Truth be told, I hadn't heard his speech slur in a while, so maybe he was getting better. I wasn't sure. My father had a well-trained poker face; it was hard to tell when he was lying and when he wasn't. I was just happy to believe. I had one more thing I wanted to ask him.

'Dad, you know when you went in with the fake ID to get Uncle Thanh and Uncle Huy out of the re-education camp? How come you weren't scared then?' He laughed hysterically. 'Is that what people say about me, Anh?

'Yeah, pretty much . . . like on the boat with the pirates and all the other times. Everyone reckons you have no fear.'

HAHAHAHAHAHAHAHA! He was enjoying this immensely.

'Let them believe it, son. But if you really want to know the truth, I was shitting myself! All of the those times . . . shitting myself!' *Hahaha.* 'Just don't let the bastards know you're scared, then conquer them.'

Jesus. He was scared all those times, and yet he still managed to pull it all off. In that moment my respect and love for this man went up tenfold.

• Eleven •

All through my childhood my father taught me how to handle animals.

'Don't see them as animals, Anh, see them as young children. Many animals are as smart as a two-year-old child', he would say.

I had no idea my animal handling skills would land me my first ever regular acting role on a TV show.

In 2002, they began casting for a children's show called *Don't Blame Me*, a modern-day take on *Skippy*. It was an English–Australian co-production and it featured lots of kangaroos, koalas, crocodiles, and the like. It was about an English family who came out to live in Australia after they inherited a wildlife park that needed a lot of love. The producers wanted me to try out for the role of a park ranger named Vinnie. I was so grateful to them for creating a non-stereotypical role. Here was a Vietnamese-born expert on Australian animals, an Asian Steve Irwin. I really wanted this job. I already knew how I would audition for the part.

On the day of the audition, I walked in with Rocky, my budgie, sitting on my head and said hi to the casting agent. She took one look at the bird, screamed, and ran out of the room.

'What the hell just happened?' I stood there, shocked.

A man walked in and saw the look on my face.

'Sorry about that', he said matter-of-factly. 'Christine has a bird phobia. I'll do the audition with you. Not your fault. You weren't to know.'

This is going well, I thought.

So we started reading the lines, and it was as if Rocky knew what was going on. He was the perfect cast mate. I'd turn to him and kept throwing him lines.

'What do you say, Rocky? Shall we go help?' And right on cue he'd start chirping away like he understood me.

'Where are the kids?'

Chirp, chirp.

'In the old abandoned mine?'

Chirp, chirp.

'And tunnel twelve has collapsed due to the inherent structural weakness of the original ferric iron?'

Chirp, chirp.

The agent and producers loved it. I got the part, and Christina sent me a card: 'Sorry I freaked out, I do have a phobia.'

The show was a wonderful experience and Dad used to love watching it, seeing me using the animal handling skills he'd taught me as a kid. One day I had to act with a carpet python that was three metres long. We had a professional snake handler who passed me the snake and reassured me about other basic facts.

'He went to the toilet yesterday, which means he's good for another month or so', he said.

A month? Phwoar. Imagine what a month's worth of snake poos would smell like. I hadn't even thought about a snake having bodily functions but was relieved to hear that his system was okay.

As we did the scene, I felt this slick of wetness roll down my back.

'Ughh! Something stinks', the actor playing opposite me sniffed. Then I saw the camera man and sound operator pointing at me, unable to decide if it was horrific or hysterical.

'Oh, dude! That snake's shitting all over your back . . .'

For the record, a month's worth of snake poo is the worst smell on planet Earth.

You lying bastard, I thought to myself, looking around for the snake handler who was suddenly nowhere in sight. The crew were wetting themselves as I took a quick shower, changed into a new shirt and re-shot the scene. I couldn't wait to go home and use Mum's back-scrubbing brush for a full thirty minutes to get the stench off me.

Mum and Dad always told us kids to, 'Do as much as you can to give back to this beautiful country that gave us a second chance'. So we all do a fair bit of charity work.

In 2003 my brother Khoa and I volunteered for a charity called Open Family, and they decided to start up a ten-week course of drama classes for 'at risk street youth'. It was basically going to be a couple of hours a week. The kids would make a ten-minute video, which would be a bit of fun and help boost their self-esteem. But once they got into it, the kids—being kids—didn't want to make a ten-minute video, they wanted to make a feature film.

Part of me loved their have-a-go attitude.

'It's all well and good that they want to make a movie', I said to Khoa when we were talking about it, 'but feature films cost a few million dollars, and we've got a budget of $340'.

'These are amazing kids, Anh', Khoa said to me. 'They've lived extraordinary lives, some had been street kids for a long time, others were on parole. They all have amazing stories to tell.'

So it was Khoa who convinced me that it was worth giving this a go. With a starting budget of $340, we set out to make a feature film. Khoa would direct the film, I was going to help him produce it.

'To thine own self be true'—our humble mother's words of wisdom. We followed our instincts and an amazing serendipitous chain of events occurred that gave a bunch of street kids and their first-time director and producer a chance at making a movie.

The local paper got wind of this great little project and did a write up about us, providing a phone number for anyone who wanted to be involved. The next day we got a whole lot of phone calls from people who wanted to help out; from volunteers to fresh film graduates willing to lend their services. The most amazing phone call was from the owner of the local pub who called up and offered to sponsor us with $5000, on one condition: he got to be called executive producer.

'Sir', I said to him, 'for your $5000, we'll call you whatever you want'.

A year and a half later we released the film, calling it *The Finished People*. We gave it this title because many of the street kids referred to themselves as 'finished people' as they thought that their lives were as good as over. Our feature-length film played at proper theatres and everything. Margaret Pomeranz and David Stratton from *The Movie Show* reviewed it and both of them gave it four and half stars out of a possible five. Margaret called it 'one of the best Australian films of the year'. We got nominated and won a whole bunch of film industry awards and it really was one of the most amazing experiences I've ever had. Little did I know it would lead on to the happiest day of my mum's life.

I'd always had a great relationship with my brother Khoa—even after his Siamese fish got mine pregnant. After working so closely with him on the film, I realised just how special a person he really was. I watched as he mentored these street kids; looked after them and took them under his wing and gave them a love and respect that they'd never experienced before in their lives, not even from their own families. One of the kids came up to me one day and told me that if it wasn't for Khoa, he would've committed suicide five times over. *Wow.*

Seeing how beautifully Khoa looked after these kids, combined with his generosity in giving and helping charities in general, I thought I'd nominate him for what is probably the greatest award that a kid in Australia can win: Young Australian of the Year.

In the beginning it was really just a way of patting him on the back and saying, 'I reckon you've done great, bro!' It turned out that I wasn't the only one who thought he'd done enormously well.

The phone rang and Suzie answered it.

'It's Khoa. He sounds angry.'

I got on the phone and Khoa did sound annoyed.

'Oh man, I've bloody won New South Wales.'

'Yeah, how good's that?' I said, feigning innocence.

He was now one of eight finalists for the big national award. At the start of the whole thing, when I called Khoa up and told him that I had nominated him, he laughed for a bit then said, 'What? You're joking aren't you?' I could tell that he was uncomfortable with it. I tried to soothe him.

'It's a real long shot, Khoa. Just a bit of fun, you know.'

'Thanks, Anh. But it is a long shot, aye.'

He said this to reassure himself. Khoa loves doing good things, but he hates being acknowledged for it. He hates show-offs, he hates fanfare, he hates fakes. The only reason he went along with it was because he thought he had as much chance of winning the award as Jean Claude Van Damme has of winning an Oscar. So when he won the state finals and became one of the favourites to win the big national award, I had a lot of explaining to do.

'Khoa, wait. It's a good thing.'

'How? I'd just rather do my thing, and someone else can get the awards and do all that ra ra, "I'm so great", rubbish.'

'Khoa, I know you just want to do good things for people. If you win, you can do *more* good for *more* people. The Young Australian of the Year gets more meetings and phone calls than Khoa Do from some charity. So more kids will benefit from your work.'

'Okay, but if I win the whole thing, you're dead meat.'

So, there we were—Australia Day, 26 January 2005. Mum, Tram, Suzie and I found ourselves in the nation's capital at a ceremony with thousands of people awaiting the announcement of the Australians of the year. We were in the VIP section where family members of finalist were allowed to sit. Khoa came over and pulled me aside. He had a huge grin on his face.

'I never thought I'd be happy to be here.'

'Yeah?' I wondered what had changed.

'The last couple of weeks . . . I'm starting to realise what a massive deal this is, and umm . . . thanks for putting my name in.'

'Wouldn't it be cool if you won?'

'That would be very cool', he said.

He punched me on the shoulder and I saw a twinkle in his eyes that said, 'I love you, bro'. That made me want to hug him and tell him how much I loved him back. Of course, being a bloke, I just punched him back. Harder.

Mum was jumping out of her skin. We had a chat the night before about how great it would be if Khoa won, but how he had done so well already that we were going to celebrate no matter what.

'Doesn't matter!' Mum said, just like when I went for school captain or when Khoa and I sat for those scholarships.

There were a bunch of speeches and then the prime minister stepped up to the microphone.

'The 2005 Young Australian of the Year is . . . Khoa Do!'

Jesus Christ! Khoa's done it. My brother just won Young Australian of the Year.

Khoa, the baby dangled over the side of the boat by the pirates, the toddler that Mum dressed in little girls' dresses, the fat kid who thought the homeless woman was going to eat him . . . had just won Young Australian of the Year.

Mum was bawling tears of happiness. So was I. So was everyone.

After the wildlife park show *Don't Blame Me* finished, I got offered little one-off bit parts in Australian dramas like *All Saints*, and I discovered I really enjoyed acting. I guess it was a deep fondness that began way back in high school with Mrs Borny's secret drama classes.

I was keen to act some more, but roles really were quite rare for an Asian face like mine, so I thought, *Bugger this, I'll create my own.* I sat down and within a couple of months wrote a feature film for myself to star in called *Footy Legends*. My brother Khoa and my wife Suzie helped re-write it, and a few years later we had funding and backing from Mel Gibson's company, Icon, and were ready to go.

The movie was about a bunch of down-and-out friends from Sydney's outer suburbs who entered a local rugby league competition to try to get their lives back on track. I played the lead character, Luc, who was trying to find a job while bringing up a little sister on his own.

Having been on *The Footy Show* a number of times, I'd met a lot of the greatest players in rugby league history. So I got on the phone and asked a bunch of them if they wanted to be in the film. It was a long shot, but I just thought I'd try. Amazingly, every single player said yes, and we ended up with cameos from players like Brett Kenny, Brad Clyde and Cliffy Lyons.

What a coup! These guys were all-time legends. If it had been a soccer film this would have been the equivalent of having Maradona, Pele and Beckham in your movie.

The best part of *Footy Legends* was having my whole family join in the making of it. Apart from Khoa and I, Mum acted in a few key scenes and my sister, Tram, was the photographer for the shoot. Suzie played the part of a nurse in the film. She carried a small curly-haired boy with a bandage around his head—this was our son, Xavier, who was two at the time, so it was indeed a huge family effort.

Over three freezing winter months we filmed this little battler Australian comedy that wore its heart on its sleeve. I am incredibly proud of it. There isn't a week goes by that I don't have someone, from a kid to an old lady, come up and say to me, '*Footy Legends* . . . I loved it'.

Well, I loved making the film, and truly had the time of my life. There was only one moment during the whole process where I could have gotten myself into serious trouble.

In the opening scene I had to come out of a river with a turtle I'd just caught in my hands. It would go on to become a pet for my little sister in the film. It was quite a starring role for a reptile. We scoured all of Australia and found that, believe it or not, there was indeed an acting turtle, called Bob. I met him and it was clear that Bob thought he was a human. He stuck his head out to look at you, gave you kisses and even had little turtle chats with you. Bob was perfect, and really the only option because turtles naturally bury their heads inside their shells when people pick them up. Without Bob, it would've looked like my little sister was keeping an empty shell for a pet.

The day we filmed the scene of me 'catching' Bob turned out to be the coldest day of the previous three years. We rocked up to Georges River National Park at 7 a.m. and it was so bitterly freezing I would have happily spoon-cuddled my mate Steve again. My task was to simply submerge myself in the water, holding Bob, act as if I'd just caught him, and then pop out holding him triumphantly in the air! *Easy peasy*.

I prepared myself mentally—my motivation: 'catch the turtle, catch the turtle'—and then Bob's owner/agent passed him to me and I jumped into the water. Immediately my breath was taken away and my entire body screamed for me to get out. My teeth chattered and I shivered uncontrollably, but I swam to the middle of the river using just one arm because my other hand was holding a turtle.

The director, my brother Khoa, called 'Action!' and I went under. As soon as I was submerged, both my legs cramped up. I couldn't move properly and was thrashing about desperately with my non-turtle holding arm. It was no use and I started to sink.

It was an interesting dilemma I was faced with: Do I let go of Bob and save myself, or do I hang on till someone saves me? A little voice inside piped up, *Hold on to the turtle or it will swim away up the river. Don't lose the only acting turtle in all of Australia.* So I continued to flail about like a one-armed, legless torso.

On the riverbank, Khoa said to his assistant, 'Geez, Anh's over-acting'. He shouted to me, 'Anh, just go down and come up, holding the turtle'.

'Help, help', I shouted. Khoa looked pissed off.

'Tone it down, Anh, this isn't the time for ad-libs.' I looked up at him, all snuggled up in a blanket, with a heater, and his continuity girl handing him a skinny latté.

'Cramp, cramp!' I called out. The safety man standing on the river's edge could see I was in trouble and he jumped in and saved me. I got out of the water and gave Bob back to his owner. Khoa was laughing his head off.

'I thought you were over-acting!'

HAHAHAHAHAHAHAHA.

Footy Legends was the turning point. Phone calls started coming in soon after it was released. First, it was *Thank God You're Here*. The producer called my manager and said, 'We want Anh'.

What a moment. It's a show that many comedians watched at home and said to themselves, *I wonder if I'd be any good at that?* It's at once a performer's ultimate dream and worst nightmare. The basic concept is that they throw you into the middle of a scene where you're the only one who's completely unprepared. You step through a door and someone says, 'Thank god you're here'. From there you play the scene as if you know what the hell's going on, with a live studio audience watching, expecting, actually demanding, you to be funny.

I have always prided myself on being well prepared with my comedy material, but to go on a show watched by millions with a totally blank script was like jumping out of an aeroplane without a parachute and then quickly knitting one on the way down.

'Tell them I don't want to do it', I said to my manager.

'Anh, I'm not going to say that to them now, I'm going to call you back tomorrow, let you sleep on it.' My manager Andrew is a smart operator and knows me well. He knew my commonsense would override the initial fear.

'So you going to do it, Anh?' he asked the next day.

'Yes! Oh my god, tell them yes.'

I went on the show and with a bit of beginner's luck, won the trophy for the best performance. I've since been invited back three times and people have often asked me whether it gets any easier. The answer? No. Hell, no. And oh my sweet lord, no.

Just as I'd started thinking, *Right, I've done a gig in front of two hundred war veterans, I've done* Thank God You're Here, *nothing will ever scare me again,* Andrew rang.

'Anh, they want you to be on *Dancing with the Stars.*'

I felt like I was my old corella, Pacino, and Andrew had just said 'Poo!'

I rushed home to tell Suzie. Her response was pure loving honesty.

'You can't dance!'

'I know!'

Several factors are important here. Firstly, I really can't dance. Secondly, I have a short attention span. Thirdly ... what was I talking about again? Anyway I now faced my greatest professional challenge yet. If the terror of *Thank God You're Here* was having nothing prepared, the challenge of *Dancing with the Stars* was exactly the opposite: having to remember three hundred and forty-seven steps as well as arm, neck, head, foot and elbow positions during each step. *Ahhhh!*

The only saving grace for me was that they teamed me up with a five-time world salsa champion, Luda Kroitor. She was a battle hardened, *Dancing with the Stars* veteran, having taken several actors past half way and world boxing champion Kostya Tszyu to the grand final.

'Sorry you got me', I said to her when we met.

'Nonsense! Show me what you can do.'

She had this thick Russian accent and a wonderful direct manner about her. She grabbed me and we tried out few moves.

'Oh my god, you are right . . . you are bad.'

We started practising about a month before the first episode and somehow she got me into pretty decent shape for a guy who's best move at a dance club had been the 'drunk grandad side-to-side shuffle'.

'As long as we don't get kicked out the first week, I'm happy', I said to Luda. 'Anything after that is a bonus.'

We did better than just surviving the first week. Improving slowly but surely, we somehow found ourselves past half way.

It was round about week six when I went to visit some kids at the Westmead Children's Hospital. Every celebrity on the show supports a charity and mine was the Day of Difference Foundation set up by the family of Sophie Delizio, the brave little girl who was twice seriously injured in tragic events. Whenever I got a home viewer vote, a portion of the call cost went towards buying medical equipment for children's hospitals.

As I drove there I steeled myself. I am absolutely hopeless when it comes to sick children. My wife tells me I freak out and become a useless worrier when my little boys get so much as a slight sniffle. When I have MC'd events in the past for charities like Kids with Cancer, they sometimes played videos of a battling child's journey, which sometimes ends happily, but most often doesn't. I always lost composure.

I met a bunch of kids that day including a little eight-year-old boy, Adam, who suffered from a rare disease that struck him suddenly, damaging his spinal cord and paralysing him from the neck down. Up until a few months earlier he was just a kid running round, kicking a footy, then all of a sudden he was fighting for his life.

Little Adam was lying there and his mother told me, 'I get my strength from him'. This kid was so weak and tired, but he still tried with all his might to cheer up his worried mum by making her laugh. Adam had been in hospital for a couple of months and was battling this severe disease bravely.

I pulled out some magic tricks, gave him a small toy and we filmed the segment. After I said goodbye I rushed to my car and sat there, crying my eyes out. I thought about Adam, whose big smile reminded me of my own sons' big grins, and then I thought about Adam's mother. What would I be going through in her place? You could see that her terror at the thought of her boy dying was only barely masked by her strength as a mum. She was desperately trying to hold back the tears for her son's sake.

She reminded me of my own mother and a story that my aunties had told me so many times before. When we were on the boat coming to Australia, there was a point where I was sick from dehydration. I was lying very still, my lips cracked dry and my face gaunt from vomiting and diarrhoea. What I needed was water, clean water. Although we were in the middle of the ocean, there was not a drop to drink. My mother faced losing her son, and she held and rocked me all through the night, singing me lullabies and praying for a miracle to happen.

I sat in my car and felt overwhelmed by a deep and profound sense of gratitude for my life and for my mother. I drove straight from the hospital to the dance studios.

'We've been doing four hours of dance practice a day', I said to Luda. 'Let's bump it up to eight.'

'Okay. Let's do it. What happened to lazy guy?'

'I just realised how lucky I am.'

'What do you mean?'

'Nothing. Let's go.'

Up until that point I was just mucking around. It's in my nature to take it easy and have a laugh. I'd survived the first round of eliminations, so I was now in bonus territory. Every week I found myself in the bottom two so the end was probably close. It seemed like the judges were going to score me low anyway. But now I had a reason to stick around as long as I could.

I started to train as hard as possible, and it began to pay dividends. I started climbing up the rankings and a few weeks later I topped the scores, which sent me into the grand final. I was shocked, my family were shocked, the judges were traumatised.

Everywhere I went total strangers were wishing me luck, and it was a strange feeling. For most of the series the judges had slaughtered me in the scoring. Fair enough, I guess, I'm really not that great a dancer. So when I reached the grand final, I realised it was because the Australian public had voted for me. The judges' vote was worth fifty per cent and the home viewers' vote was worth the other fifty. It was a revelation. This funny looking Vietnamese kid was getting voted through each week by the Australian public. That said a lot about what a wonderful country this is. It melted away all those moments in my life, and there have been very few to be honest, when I'd copped racism and had been made to feel like an outsider.

In the grand final episode I had to learn three dances in one week. *Sheesh!* It was a lot to ask a guy who was not that talented a dancer and had a short attention span. I was up against Bridie Carter, an actress from *McLeod's Daughters*, who had won a Gold Logie for Most Popular TV Personality in Australia. Added to this, she was an amazing dancer who scored tens just about every single week. It was a tall ask.

Alas, I tried as hard as I could, but I was beaten by a better dancer, a much better dancer and a friend. Throughout the series Bridie and I had got to know each other and it was like competing with a best mate.

'Doesn't matter!' squealed my mum, who had the house full of uncles and aunties and friends all cheering for their little Vietnamese boy who very nearly lost his life on a boat, but had just made them proud on the grand final of *Dancing with the Stars*.

One of the greatest delights of being on the show was the joy it brought to my family. My mum used to get everyone over and throw 'Anh's on *Dancing*' parties. They just loved seeing me being a funny bugger on TV and being acknowledged by the whole country. Mum would be walking through Bankstown shops and Vietnamese women would say, 'Your boy, oh my god, he's so good! We voted for him.' Every week Mum put twenty or thirty votes in for me herself.

'Stop wasting your money, it's not going to make a difference', I told her.

'I know it doesn't, I just want to do it', she replied. I realised that it wasn't about making a difference to me staying in or not, it was about her being able to support her son, so every week she registered multiple votes. Mum also reasoned that the votes were contributing to a charity and that made it a win–win for her.

At the same time Dad was throwing *Dancing* parties in Melbourne. He'd buy a couple of slabs of beer and invite twenty friends over. They told me later that, every time I danced, my father would get up and do the funky chicken. It's like someone showed him this one dance move and it's all he had in his repertoire. Everyone would whoop and cheer at both of us, and then swear and throw empty cans at the judges when they gave me a bad score.

Then there was Grandma. In week four of the competition I danced the waltz and dedicated it to her. She had seen me on TV plenty of times, but she'd never understood my jokes with her limited English. However, costumes and music and beautiful movement was something she truly loved—remember this was the grandma who would come home after a day in the garden, crack open a beer and sing a few hours of karaoke. *Dancing with the Stars* quickly became her favourite show, and she would look forward to it every week, counting the days till she would see, 'My beautiful Anh' dancing on TV again.

One thing that concerned her, however, was all the weight I was losing. My grandma is one of these eat-up-good-have-some-more type of women. After struggling to feed ten children in bitter poverty, she came to Australia and discovered a land of plentiful food. When I was young all my mates loved coming over to our place because my mum and grandma would send them home a few kilograms heavier, filled up with wonderful exotic foods from spring rolls to egg custard tarts.

I started *Dancing* weighing eighty-five kilograms. Over the three months of the show, doing between four and eight hours of dance training a day, I lost a total of thirteen kilos. When I'd reached seventy-two kilograms none of my clothes fit anymore, so towards the end of the series I was turning up to Channel 7 studios in the only thing that wouldn't fall off my waist, my Year 10 school pants.

I was so happy with my new trim figure that I went and gave all my bigger clothes to St Vincent de Paul and bought a whole new wardrobe. Of course, as soon as *Dancing* finished I packed on those thirteen kilos again in the following three months. I went back to Hornsby St Vincent de Paul to try and buy my chunky clothes back and couldn't find a single item. I really should've taken Uncle Dung because there were heaps of cheap fur coats.

Being on reality TV is an interesting experience. The audience watch you be yourself because you let your guard down, and people get to know you pretty well. Sometimes they kind of expect you to be familiar with them too.

A week after the series had finished, I was in the bank paying off my credit card, holding about eight hundred cash in my hands. Suddenly an arm grabbed me from behind. I went into I'm-being-mugged mode and my mind frantically went, *Kick him in the shins, poke him in the eyes, stomp on his* . . . The arm spun me round, and it was an old lady.

'Tango with me, Anh!' I was so surprised, and relieved. I shuffled around with her as the bank staff chuckled.

'I voted for you, Anh', she said. I realised how absurd and wonderful it was that total strangers had spent money to keep me in a dancing show, and I will never know who you all are, but I will forever be grateful. Thank you.

One day I was walking down the street and a man approached me. It took me a brief moment to recognise him, after all I hadn't seen him in almost twenty years.

'Anh! Do you remember Uncle?'

'Uncle Six.' I put out my hand and shook his awkwardly.

'I've been watching you on TV. Very good. Very good.' That familiar smile, his white teeth piercing through his dark skinned face.

'Thanks, thanks . . . umm, good to see you again', I muttered and with that I walked off, resisting the urge to turn back and give him a huge hug, buy him a beer and catch up on twenty years with my once-favourite uncle, the one who was like a second dad to me. But instead I brushed him off. At the time I thought I had good reason. I had once sat up late talking to Dad and somehow we got talking about Uncle Six.

'He's a dickhead, Anh.' Dad started telling me how a few years earlier Grandma had seen Uncle Six in the street, and how he had looked down at his feet and pretended not to see her at all. He just walked right on by.

'Grandma took him in when his mum was too poor to look after him, and after raising him up, what does he do? He pisses off and never even rings to see how she's doing. Even ignores her on the street.' My father is very protective of Grandma, and so am I. So when I'd seen him that day, the first thing that came up in my mind was, *You bastard*. I'd loved my uncle, but I love my grandma more.

Then when I began researching this book, I interviewed my grandma and found out something that broke my heart. Indeed, Uncle Six had been an adopted boy, but there was something else that no one in the family had ever been told. Something that my grandma had kept secret until she told me, and gave me permission to put into this book. Grandma told me that Uncle Six was the lovechild of her husband.

What?

'Your grandfather . . .' she stumbled, wiping away tears as the memories came back to her. 'Your grandfather had an affair with a woman during his time as a soldier. One day he comes back with this boy and he tells me everything that happened, and he asks me to adopt this boy as if he were our own.'

'Oh my god. Weren't you angry?'

'Of course I was. But this boy's mother was so poor. He would've starved to death.'

'Does my dad know?'

'No. Nobody knows. Everyone just thinks he's some poor boy we adopted.'

I fumbled with my little dictaphone that I had been using to record our conversation. 'Just give me a minute—I'll erase it from the tape.'

'No don't erase it, Anh.' She grabbed my hand and said, 'I want you to tell everyone. I need for him to be forgiven. I need for him to forgive me. I need for this to be told.'

'I can't tell them. You tell them Grandma.'

'You tell them for me.'

'I . . . I'm not equipped with all the facts. They'll slay me.'

'Then let them all find out when they read your book.'

And so, to all my uncles and aunties and my extended family . . . ahhh . . . surprise!

A Channel 7 producer called up and asked me if I wanted to go on *Celebrity Deal or No Deal*.

'Why not?'

It was during *Dancing with the Stars*, and Channel 7 was doing a cross promotion, so they invited five of us who were already on *Dancing* to do a week on *Deal or no Deal*, which they called *Dancing with the Deals*. We weren't playing for ourselves, we were playing on behalf of lucky home viewers.

The morning I was due on the show I woke up from a dream where I picked case number twenty-three, and it had $200 000 in it. So there I am, my first time on a game show, and host Andrew O'Keefe turned and asked me, 'Which case, Anh?'

'Andrew I had a dream about case twenty-three. So let's go with that.'

So case twenty-three got placed in the middle of the studio unopened. It was now my case, and wouldn't get opened until the end. We started opening up the other cases.

I was playing pretty well, *wham, wham, wham*, and I was feeling pretty good, like this was easy, like there was that thing they called 'flow' happening. After all, I'd had a dream.

We got to the end of the episode, and there was only one single case left to open. Andrew looked at me.

'Anh, you crazy kid, the bank is offering a guaranteed $125 000. Do you want to risk that to go for the $200 000?'

I had heard beforehand that in the history of the show in Australia, over nearly one thousand episodes, only one person had ever won the top prize. I thought about it.

I have a fifty-fifty chance here of winning $200 000, what the hell do I do?

Just then my father's voice was inside my head: 'There's now and there's too late, son—give it a crack and see what happens!'

Shut up, Dad! Here I was, having a conversation with my father in my head, while I was filming a TV show.

The crowd couldn't believe I was even thinking about it. 'Take the deal!' they screamed. I looked around and they were all saying the same thing : 'Take the deal, take the deal!'

Now or too late. You guys aren't me. I turned to Andrew.

'I had a dream, Andrew. Let's go for it.'

The drum roll came on, I walked over to my case, flicked open the latch and opened it up to reveal—*$200 000!*

WHOO-HOOO!!!!!!

The audience were on their feet, going bananas. I've never had another dream come true in my life. I just stood there in ecstasy.

But here's the best bit. The show was pre-filmed, and about two months later it was about to go to air and someone at Channel 7 called me up.

'Anh, you want to know who that $200 000 is going to go to?'

I said, 'Tell me'.

The producer was so excited, like she couldn't wait to tell me. 'Well the most amazing thing has happened. A totally independent body that draws the home viewer winner with a computer, has randomly picked a young man called Daniel Martin. Daniel is a stay-at-home carer for his wife who has a hole in her heart. They have two kids, six and four years old, and they live in housing commission.'

Wow.

'Anh, can you fly down to Melbourne to film a story for *Today Tonight?*'

'Of course I can.'

I hung up the phone and looked up into the heavens. I was elated, I was happy, I was moved. But I wasn't at all surprised. I had dreamed it. I didn't see the name of the winner in my dream, but I remember waking up with a feeling like I'd won it for a poor, battling family.

So there I was, in working-class Broadmeadows, in the outer suburbs of Melbourne, and huddled next to me was Andrew O'Keefe, the host of *Deal or No Deal*. It must've been a peculiar sight, two very well-known adult men crouching behind some spindly bushes outside a tiny little fibro shack, each holding one end of a four-foot-long TV cheque with $200000 written on it. Like lottery secret agents.

'We've got to move back a bit', I said to Andrew, 'otherwise they'll see us in the reflection off that adjacent window'. I was good at hiding around houses, lots of training from all those times when the landlord came to collect the late rent, and Khoa, Tram and I would hide from him. This time I was hiding to surprise a family not with a threat of eviction or violence, but to hand them two hundred grand.

Inside the house the TV crew were filming Daniel Martin and his wife Sarah, watching me on *Deal or No Deal*. The couple had gotten their nanna to look after the kids so it was just the two of them sitting there on their little couch trembling, sweating, gasping in horror every time I risked another larger sum of money.

The producers had told the couple I was representing them, but had not said what I'd won. This poor couple were watching a crazy impulsive comedian risking their money, in figures so large they had never in their life contemplated having.

It got to the end of the episode, the bit where I decided to risk a $125000, and Daniel and Sarah were holding each other tightly. Sarah had her head buried into Daniel's shoulder, and she was trembling like a three-year-old child after a nightmare. She was shaking so much it was disturbing. I think to myself, *Anh you idiot, she's got a weak heart!* A big surprise is fun, but I really didn't want anyone dying.

They watch me open the case . . . *BOOM!*

Two hundred thousand dollars!

Daniel and Sarah just hugged each other in complete silence, except for the occasional sound of a young couple sobbing. Andrew and I walked in through the front door—the two grown men who had been hiding in the bushes had now turned into two grown men trying very hard not to cry. We handed them the big cheque and Daniel gave me a hug, his tears wetting my ear and my neck.

'Thank you, Anh. We've got the money to look after Sarah now . . . my wife's going to be okay now . . . thank you.'

People often asked me afterwards, 'If you had known you were playing for that poor family, would you have risked it?'

'Of course not!'

I would've stopped at a few thousand bucks. I really would have stopped much sooner.

Others asked me: 'If you were playing for you and not a home viewer, would you have risked it?'

'Absolutely . . . There's only two times in life, there's now, and there's too late.'

Channel 7 were hosting the Beijing Olympics coverage and offered me my first solo show. It was a one-hour-long travelogue-style program. Over three weeks I visited a bunch of different cities in China to get up to silly business.

We stopped off at a rural restaurant and I asked the owner (via my interpreter) for the best delicacy in the house. He took me out the back where he had a hidden basket. He opened it up and there was a dark writhing ball of black snakes. He grabbed one and, without warning me, chopped its head off. I watched a still 'alive' head wriggling on the ground, looking at me, and almost fainted. I then got ushered over to a table in the restaurant and soon the stir-fried snake with black bean sauce was brought out. I tried it and it was fine, a bit like really tough fish, but actually quite tasty.

Then the owner put a shot glass in front of me and it contained a little green jelly sort of thing inside some rice wine.

'Drink it, drink it', he said smiling.

I'll just knock this back, it'll be like an oyster and I won't be able to taste it, I thought. Just before I went to pick it up, however, the owner grabbed a chopstick and poked the 'thing'. A thick green slime oozed out of it. I turned to the camera, flashed my best TV smile, and quickly swallowed the whole glass in one quick movement, like a tequila shot.

'Hmm. That's no so baaa . . .' But I couldn't even finish the word, I felt the contents of my stomach shoot up my throat. I clamped my mouth shut, covered it with both hands, then looked around furiously and ran to the nearest window, where I violently threw up, just missing a goat outside. My body screamed at me: *No good, Anh, no good at all . . .*

The owner of the restaurant and his wife laughed their heads off.

'What was in the glass?' I asked them.

'Snake gallbladder.' I suppressed my disgust.

'Was it a joke?'

'No, for real. It helps 'men's issues', you know?' the owner winked and nudged me in the ribs.

When I got back home I said to Suzie, 'If I ever have 'manhood problems' when we're in China, well, sorry sweetheart, but you're missing out because I'm never drinking snake gallbladder again.'

Because my crew was with Channel 7, the Olympic broadcaster, we were given passes into the Olympic compound. At the time, about two months before the games started, no one in the outside world had seen the inside of the Birds Nest stadium. As we drove into the compound, about a thousand Chinese males, ranging from ten year olds to adults, marched in, all dressed in white. They were rehearsing for the Opening Ceremony. *Awesome.*

'Film this!' I called out to the cameraman as I hopped out of our car and found a row of guys about my height, then quickly slipped in and began marching with them. Apart from the fact that they were all wearing white and my shirt was blue, I fitted in perfectly. The Chinese marchers either side of me snuck a look, but didn't know what to do, so they kept going. Because there was a cameraman filming me, they must have thought I was an official, or at least part of the spectacle in some way.

We got through the first bunch of guards. My heart was thumping. *I've just pulled a Chaser-style stunt in a communist country*, I thought to myself.

There were ten guards around, and they all had pistols and rifles and serious looks on their faces. We approached the very last checkpoint. After that we were inside the Birds Nest! Me and the cameraman.

What do we do? Pull out before we get a look inside the Birds Nest, but save ourselves from arrest and preserve a month's worth of footage, or have a crack? It was a no-brainer. In we went. We didn't get far.

'Excuse me, sir. Who are you? Where's your paperwork?' the guard asked in halting English as he put out a long arm. I kept a straight face.

'I'm the warm-up guy.' He smiled, so I kept going.

'I'm Jackie Chan's body double.' The guard laughed and I decided to show him a magic trick, and pulled a red hanky out of nowhere. He wasn't impressed.

'No, sorry, can't go in.' A shame. Maybe if the trick had been better . . .

I patted him on the back and walked away. It had ended okay. But there was a moment there when I thought to myself, *I really could end up in a Gobi Desert jail.* Then another part of me thought . . . *No problem, I know a bloke who'll steal some fake IDs and bust me out.*

Just like me, my dad loves sports. He loves seeing people going all in and, throwing the dice for that one shot at glory. So when SBS asked me to host a sports quiz show called *The Squiz*, I was rapt. Hosting *The Squiz*, for me, was like being a kid in a candy shop. Every week I met sports stars and listened to them share amazing experiences, which many people—myself included—had never heard about.

Aussie Joe Bugner, the former heavyweight boxer, came on and told us about the first time he fought Muhammad Ali. It was in Las Vegas in 1973. Three days before the fight, Bugner got into the hotel lift. It went up to the mezzanine, the doors opened and there, standing right in front of him, was Ali. Ali walked in, and the two of them were alone in the lift. Ali began trash-talking Bugner and started throwing a flurry of punches at him, stopping half a centimetre in front of his nose. The lift carried them up to the twenty-sixth floor and Ali got out.

'The fight was as good as over', said Bugner. 'I was completely intimidated from that moment on. For the next three days I lived in fear of the man.' That's how Bugner told it; a fantastic story. When the episode aired I watched it with Dad, and afterwards pulled out a little piece of paper and gave it to him. It read 'Get well soon Anh's dad.' Signed: 'Aussie Joe Bugner'.

I also appeared on *Top Gear Australia*, which is an Aussie version of the popular BBC driving show. Part of being the guest for that week was doing the 'hot lap' in the hero vehicle. My cousins said to me, 'Anh, we're sick of the stereotype that Asians can't drive, you gotta go on the show and blow that out of the water'.

Sweet, I thought. *I'm going to floor it, the pedal's going to be rammed so hard against the metal the two of 'em are going to be like conjoined twins.*

I turned up to an airport where they filmed the hot lap and I'm raring to go.

'Here's the car, Anh.' I jumped inside all pumped up and then I looked down.

'Oh my god, it's a manual.'

I'd never driven a manual before and I couldn't even get it to start. The producer of the show came over and decided to give me a couple of quick lessons. We filmed what must surely be one of the slowest hot laps in *Top Gear* history, more of a tepid-to-cold lap really, as I bunny hopped my way around and finished the entire course in mostly second gear.

One of my favourite TV experiences was appearing on a show called *Thank You*. It was a Channel 7 special where people surprised someone they wanted to say a big thank you to. For example, someone was thanking a person who'd pulled them out of a burning car, and another person was thanking someone who donated an organ to them. There was a celebrity part of the show and the producers called me up and asked me if there was anyone I wanted to thank. I immediately thought of my Year 8 English teacher, Mrs Borny.

There I was, back at my old school, St Aloysius, hiding outside a classroom where Mrs Borny was inside talking to a class of boys.

'You ready, Anh?' The producer asked me.

'Give us a minute', I said as I tried to compose myself. Then in I walked with the camera crew, and I saw her again for the first time in fifteen years. She looked amazing, same beautiful smile, same glint in her eye that emanated a wonderful generosity and promised you that this little, grey-haired lady was going to believe in you and give you every chance of learning and growing.

I walked up to her, gave her an enormous hug and told her about everything she'd done for me. She held me tight around my waist and said to me, 'Anh, Anh, I'm so proud of you! So proud of you!'

She was surprised and shocked and couldn't believe that I'd even remembered her. I gave her a leather-bound copy of my *Footy Legends* movie script and told her that it was her who convinced me I could write. I also told her that I was but one of probably thousands of kids who'd she'd had an impact on through her kindness, and that she was my Robin Williams character from *Dead Poets Society*. Tears welled up in her eyes.

All through my life I have been lucky to have had supportive people to help me along the way and my wife Suzie has been my soul mate and a best friend rolled into one gorgeous package. Suzie and my three boys are the best thing about my life.

Recently my eldest boy Xavier, a five-year-old asked me, 'Dad, have you been to the moon?'

'No.'

He followed up with, 'Have you been to any other planets?'

'No.'

He said, 'Dad, I might go one day'.

I channelled my own dad and said, 'You do that Xavier. You do that 'cos you can do anything'.

My second boy, Luc, overheard this conversation and piped up:

'Dad, can we go for a ride in a rocket?'

'Well, sure we can. That sounds great.'

'Can we go today?'

'Maybe not today, Luc.'

'OK. Can we go on a bus?'

Luc was three at the time and he'd never been on a bus before so off we went.

I've spent a lot of time over the years writing jokes and comedy material, but it is impossible to top some of the things that come out of my children's mouths. Another time Suzie and I asked Luc, 'What's your favourite animal?'

'Octopus, 'cos it's got eight testicles.'

At the time of writing this book, my third boy, Leon, is six months old and is like a clone of my father, only a lot better looking. He doesn't have much hair yet, but when it does grow, hopefully it won't look like he's been sleeping on the one side all his life.

I said to Suzie, 'How about we keep having kids till we get a girl?'

'Nice try, Anh. I don't want to be like your grandmother and have ten kids.' I absolutely adore Suzie and the boys and every single day I just laugh and think to myself, *I truly am the luckiest guy in the world.*

My family and friends haven't changed and their company reminds me of how fortunate I am. However, one friend called up recently with a surprise.

'Hi, Anh. I've just done this personal development course and we're supposed to call up people in our lives who mean a lot to us. And if we have any issues with them, to tell them and be honest with them.'

This is a bit weird, I thought. 'Okay. What's on your mind?'

'I just wanted to call you up and say to you, Anh, that in the past ten years you've done very well and, to be totally honest, sometimes I feel a bit jealous. I wanted to let you know that I'm really happy for everything that you've been achieving.'

'Thanks, mate, but I've never felt any jealousy from you. You've been a hundred per cent mate, so no need to apologise.'

'Well, I'm glad I never showed it on the outside, but I felt it inside and I just wanted to let you know.'

What a top bloke. That was a huge thing to do. And it was a gift for me. It made me aware of making sure my friends and family always feel they are number one. That I remember to let them know how much I cherish them.

• Twelve •

I have been back to Vietnam three times now. The first time was back in 1998, before I was dating Suzie. Mum had always wanted to show us where we all came from, and so we set a date and started saving. It was unlike saving for anything else we'd ever saved for in the past; this time it wasn't just to pay for school fees, or to pay back some debt, this time we were putting money away for an overseas holiday! We'd never done that before and it was incredible.

So I worked double overtime at the cake shop, sorted mail till my fingers were numb, and Mum, Khoa and Tram were also working hard to help us achieve this exciting goal. It didn't take long at all, and soon we had ourselves four tickets to travel back to where this crazy, wonderful journey all began.

For my mother, this trip was nothing short of a dream come true. From the moment we arrived, her face lit up. She was just so happy. This trip was a walking, living vindication of all of Mum's effort. She had sweated and struggled and worked herself to the bone to get her children through those long, difficult years and now, for the first time, we were doing something she had dreamed about, something that her imagination had put on hold for years.

As soon as we landed and drove from the airport to the hotel, I started experiencing this weird déjà vu.

This has happened before. But how can this be? I asked myself. I had left Vietnam when I was two. But I couldn't deny that the smells were familiar and they triggered strong feelings and sensations. Vietnam is an assault on the senses. Constant noise, smells, people everywhere, so much traffic that it's hard to cross the road.

After checking into our hotel, we began walking around as a family. I had automatically assumed we would blend in. Instead, we stuck out a mile. Despite the fact that we spoke the language, the locals could tell we were tourists. It might have been our jeans, Blundstones and NRL footy jumpers.

I wanted to get around like a local, so we went to a second-hand clothing market near our hotel and I bought a range of used clothes. It was ironic, here I was in Vietnam, a third world country where we were considered wealthy, and still I went looking for my designer label of choice, Le Vincent de Paul.

Everywhere we went we saw deep poverty and there were occasionally beggars. Every one of them who came up to Mum, she would give them around the equivalent of five Australian dollars and they would thank her as if she just won them *Deal or No Deal*. Throughout the trip she gave away loads of money. Being reacquainted with the country of her birth gave her a fresh perspective on what she had created for herself, and us.

'You know, we've got nothing to worry about in Australia. Nothing to worry about at all.'

At one point we met a teenage boy who was selling postcards at a temple. He had an enormous grin and my mum said to us, 'This is Anh's skinnier twin'. In that moment I had a flash of realisation. That could've been me. Indeed, if my family hadn't embarked on that trip years ago, I could've easily ended up selling trinkets at a temple for fifty cents a piece.

We visited the Mekong Delta and Mum announced to us with great fondness, 'This is very close to where we left Vietnam on our boat'. My brother was fascinated, took out his camera and shot some photos, but then on the way back we encountered some problems.

We were on tour in a mini-bus, which had about twenty people on board—Americans (including Vietnamese Americans), Danes and Brits. At one point we were on a quiet country road that was so severely flooded we couldn't cross it. The bus driver was adamant.

'I can't take the risk of driving you across.'

What the hell do we do? We couldn't go back, so our options were either to go forward or stay in the bus overnight and take our chances with the big monsoons looming in the distance. Every single passenger wanted us to go forward, but the poor little driver didn't want to be responsible for twenty tourists going missing in the Mekong River. For some reason, everyone on board turned to me.

'Anh, you get up and drive and get us across', one old man said.

But I'm only twenty-two. What about all these grown-ups? We'd been together for a week, chatted and gotten to know each other, and for some reason these people had made up their mind: Anh will drive us across.

'C'mon, Anh, we don't want to spend the night here! Drive us across!' A woman called out. So Mum turned to me.

'Anh, you want to do this?'

I whispered in Mum's ear, 'I've never driven a bus before'.

I walked outside with a couple of men to look at the depth of the water. It seemed to be getting deeper and deeper very quickly. Every ten minutes or so a huge truck with big tyres got across easily, but watching how high the water went on these big trucks made me feel that maybe our driver was right, the water was too deep for our mini-bus to cross safely. I came up with another idea. Why not get towed across?

I went back into the bus and asked if everyone would agree to pitch in five US dollars per head, and I would offer the hundred dollars to a passing truck driver to tow us across.

'Here's a hundred bucks now, Anh!' an American guy yelled, waving some bills. 'Just get us the heck outta here! We don't want to spend the night in this bus!'

I flagged down the first truck that I thought was big enough, offered the driver the hundred and, after fifteen minutes of rigging and double rigging with chains and bolts and ropes, we were ready to be towed.

Slowly but surely we progressed through the water, all of us watching nervously out the window, realising that there would be no Westpac rescue choppers or anything that fancy if we were to be swept away. With the enormous truck pulling us across, we soon found ourselves on the other side of the flooded road.

Whoo-hooo!

There was a huge cheer from everyone as we made it safely across. This put the whole bus in the most delightful mood. Everyone just started chatting away excitedly, buoyed by a glorious sense of relief. That's when I overheard Mum talking to another Vietnamese woman.

'He's clever for a young man isn't he?' said the woman.

'Yes, he is very good at these things, just like his father', Mum replied.

It was the first time in a long time that I'd heard Mum talk about Dad in a positive light. Maybe Vietnam was affecting her.

A few years ago my mum stopped working and these days she spends her time helping to look after my three kids and my sister's daughter, and she is also studying English. She tells me almost daily, 'I am in heaven, Anh'.

Mum had always wanted to study English but never had the time, having to work multiple jobs to feed three kids. For years she watched me on TV and could hear the audience laughing, but she never understood any of my jokes. Until recently she had never been to see me do stand-up comedy.

A couple of years ago, about six months after *Dancing with the Stars* finished, Mum came and saw me at the Opera House. She had never been inside the Opera House before and as she walked through the doors she saw big posters of her little boy. I did my show, which includes a segment about my mum and how amazing she is, and then at the end of it told the crowd that she was in the audience. The sell-out crowd got to their feet in unison to give my mum a standing ovation.

I looked down at her and she was crying. I couldn't hold it either, and cried all over the Opera House microphone.

Mum has gone from never seeing her son on stage, to becoming a performer herself in a very short amount of time. As she tells people, 'Last year, I crack the big time', on the corporate speaking circuit.

I had received a call from a big company that had traditionally held an annual food and wine night for their staff and decided they wanted to add comedy into the mix. The events organiser knew I spoke about my mum's cooking in my stand-up routine.

'Is your mother really a good cook?' she asked.

'The best. She never stops. When I was a kid I thought my name was 'Taste this!''

'Excellent', the lady said. 'Can she come down with you and do some cooking during the show?'

'I'll just double-check her schedule to see if she's free.' I paused, then did that *Hmm. . . hmm . . . hmm . . .* noise you do when you're pretending to look at someone's diary.

'She is available that night.'

Next they wanted to know if Mum did any public speaking.

'She does truckloads', I lied.

I went home and told Mum, 'I can book you for some speaking. Are you up for it?'

'Yes. Will I get paid?'

'How much do you want?'

'Can you get me $50?'

'I'll see what I can do.'

I went back to the company and told them she was happy to do it.

'How much does she charge?' they asked. I kept a totally straight face.

'Two thousand a show.' The events organiser didn't even blink.

'Fine, no problem. We want two shows.' I raced home.

'Mum, they've booked you for two shows!' Mum was thrilled. 'But I didn't get you the $50.'

'Oh, well, that's okay. It'll still be fun to do it with you.'

'Mum, I got you two thousand. Per night. That's four grand.' She squealed with excitement.

'I love this speaking!'

The company was generous. They flew us down to Adelaide, then Melbourne, put us up in five-star hotels—a room each. We were chauffeur-driven and taken to fancy restaurants.

'Anh, do we have to pay for this meal?'

'Mum, you don't have to pay for anything.'

She smiled at a waitress, 'Actually, I will have dessert, please.' She then turned to me. 'I love this speaking!' She was having the time of her life.

When we were in Adelaide, Mum visited her two brothers, Uncle Huy, the preist, and Uncle Dai who owns a bakery. The show was on a Thursday night, and we were due to fly back to Sydney on the Friday. On the Saturday, my third son, Leon, was due to have his christening.

As soon as we stepped into my uncle's bakery Mum stopped still in the middle of a sentence.

'Wait a minute', she said. I could see the cogs start turning in her mind. 'I'm going to get three hundred meat pasties from your uncle's bakery and we'll take them back for the christening. He'll do it for me at the family rate', she beamed.

'Mum, how are we going to lug three hundred pasties back to Sydney?' But she waved away my doubts.

'They'll be fresh, they'll be perfect.' There was no stopping her.

'Allrighty then, Mum, whatever you want to do.'

She went out the back to see my uncle and returned with two huge boxes of pasties.

Mum was fantastic in the show. Her job was to ad-lib a few cooking spots in the middle of my performance. She showed the eighty guests how to do a lazy person's version of Peking Duck and they loved it! She was an absolute natural and a big hit.

'Next time I come, I show you how to do Vietnamese Pizza! . . . Just kidding.'

Back at the hotel afterwards, I was exhausted and getting ready for bed, when I heard a knock on my door. It was Mum looking anxious.

'Anh, I can't fit all the pasties in the fridge.'

HAHAHAHAHAHA!

We took all the alcohol out of both our mini-bars and stacked the pasties inside. Their doors still wouldn't close properly, so we moved the sofa in each room against the fridges to keep them sealed as tightly as possible. Next day, we flew out with the pasties, still cold and fresh, in the luggage racks above us. They tasted delicious the next day.

In front of a large, captive audience at the christening, Mum told the story of how she made all that money.

'All I had to do was cook for five minutes, and they put us in a beautiful hotel', she giggled. All my uncles and aunts listened excitedly. She is their champion, and they love hearing about all her success and adventures.

'Two K for five minutes?' They started calculating her hourly rate.

'You're on twenty-four thousand an hour', Uncle Dung told her. 'Can we come and cook with you? I'll do it for half the money.'

Mum walked into her new English class at the start of one semester and the teacher announced that the day's lesson was about multi-culturalism. He popped a DVD into the machine and pressed 'play'. As the film started, my mother shouted out to the class, 'That's my sons' film'.

'What do you mean?' the teacher asked, surprised.

'My sons made that film', she explained.

'Oh, very good. Let's watch shall we?' the teacher replied dismissively, probably thinking to himself, *Who's this crazy Vietnamese woman?* The other students around her didn't seem to believe her either and they all continued to watch the screen. Mum sat back quietly in her seat and bided her time.

The film reached its ending and then all of a sudden my mother appeared up on the screen—doing what she does best, cooking—in the climactic final scene. The whole class turned to her and gasped.

Mum has now appeared in all of Khoa's films—one short film and three feature films—and her friends have given her a new nickname: 'Action!' She has gone from a quiet little Vietnamese woman to a movie star amongst her migrant student buddies.

I recently saw another member of my family on TV—unexpectedly. I was watching a show on the ABC late one night that was being filmed in a mental institution, and in the background I saw a patient putting a cup of coffee into a microwave—it was Uncle Two. It was a complete shock and I rang Dad straight away.

'Yeah, that's him. He's been living there for about a year', he confirmed. I had thought he was living with my aunt, but apparently it got too hard for her to look after him and they put him in a mental institution.

Uncle Two is the father of our cousin's Joe, Manh, Tri and Martin who all lived with us on the farm and in the factory in Newtown. My quietest uncle had gone through some trauma during the war and had always been withdrawn. After he was estranged from his wife, he lived with different brothers and sisters, and for a while lived with my dad in Melbourne.

One time Dad took a three-week trip to Vietnam and when he got back to Australia I went to visit him. I noticed that Uncle Two wasn't there anymore, I also noticed that the house stank, and one bedroom in particular had its door closed.

'What's going on?' I asked Dad.

'Your uncle's gone to live with your auntie and grandma now, he just can't take care of himself anymore.'

Dad opened the door to the bedroom and it was absolutely putrid. Uncle Two had been left alone for the three weeks and during this time he had gotten so lonely that he found a nest of baby birds and raised them in his own bedroom. The birds defecated all over the room and there were feathers everywhere—in the carpet, on the curtains and stuck in the window ledges.

Even though Dad had attempted to clean out the room, it still had an overpowering stench, the indescribable smell of loneliness.

Joe is Uncle Two's eldest son. He and I had always been close since we 'escaped' that giant turtle those many years ago. When I got married, Joe was one of my groomsmen.

A few years ago Joe got married. It's customary in Vietnamese weddings for the father of the groom to give a speech, as well as the father of the bride. Joe's father was in a mental hospital and so Joe asked my dad to give a speech on his behalf.

This night was one of my dad's proudest moments. He gave a fantastic speech and afterwards, as we sat drinking, I said to him, 'Good speech, Dad. You do good wedding speeches.' He could see what I was trying to say.

'I'm very happy doing the speech, Anh. I'll probably never do one for your brother and sister.' He took a drink. 'I don't deserve to—so I'm very happy today.' We clinked glasses in a way that was a celebration of his big win today, and an acknowledgement of his regret about the yesterdays.

Later in the night Dad and I were both drunk.

'How's your mother?'

'Good', I replied.

'She's the most beautiful woman in the world. You know I still love her.'

Many years ago I had said to Khoa, 'You have to go and see Dad'.

'I don't want to', was his response, and he walked into his room and slammed the door.

I asked again several months later and got the same result.

One time, my father's health problems were so severe that I thought the end was close. I felt I had no time left, and I still had a son's promise to keep.

'You have to go. If you don't I'm gonna smash you and drag you to see him', I said to Khoa.

Still no result.

Then I realised I had to be a little smarter about it.

One day Khoa and I were having a beer.

'Hey Khoa, you know how you're the Young Australian of the Year now, you should go see the old man, take your trophy and tell him he can stick it up his arse—'cos you've done so well without him. Show him how irrelevant he was.'

A few weeks later Khoa went to see Dad. Shortly after that Tram did as well.

Like me, it took them both a while to get used to the idea. Since that day I have seen a healing in my brother and sister. It hasn't been easy and it's taken a long time, but there is a forgiveness that allows them to leave behind the anger and memories of a violent drunken father, and remember a wonderful loving father.

I was there for both reunions and watched Dad change. I saw a physical, obvious transformation of a man before my very eyes. The happiness that it brought to him was so palpable that you could see a vitality literally returning to his face, his skin, his eyes.

Six months later I went to visit Dad again. As I descended the escalator at Melbourne airport, he spotted me and literally sprinted up to me. He grabbed my son Xavier, threw him into the air and sat the little fella on his right shoulder. With his other arm Dad grabbed my head and pulled me close, giving me a kiss on the cheek.

'I'm clean, Anh', he said, burying his head into my neck. 'Doctor says I'm clean.'

An old lady nearby doesn't know what's going on but it makes her smile to see two grown men hugging and sobbing.

My father's tumour proved to be benign and eventually it responded well to treatment. His health improved slowly and it's been years since I have heard his speech suffer. He credits his recovery to seeing his children again, and has since had yet another son with his partner. So now I have two half-brothers.

That very first time I went to visit Dad many years ago, I met my half-brother who Dad named Anh, after me. My third son was born in 2009. Dad asked, 'What did you call him?' I said 'Leon, but the Vietnamese shall call him Lee'.

'That's what everyone called me', Dad said.

'I know, Dad. I named him after you.'

Only a few months ago, I realised that Mum was going to find out eventually that I'd been seeing Dad, so I thought I'd tell her. Mum surprised me with her response.

'I know you see him. Just don't tell me about it.'

'All right, well, if you're going to read the book, there's going to be a few things about him in there you might not know.'

'I know everything, Anh. He's got a new wife now and a couple more kids.'

'How'd you know?' I asked her.

'I hear things. Just don't bring him up. The bastard. I just don't want to hear about him. He's got a younger woman now, he's happy.' Then she started to walk away agitated.

'Well, not that it matters, but he said to me he still reckons you're the most beautiful woman in the world.' Her demeanour changed immediately.

'Of course. That's 'cos I am.' She faked a smile and held it for a second, and then the tears forced their way out. I hugged my dear mother as tight as I could.

It is a sunny day—warm, but not too hot, with just a slight breeze—otherwise the water is a perfect mirror. We are in Bobbin Head National Park, a beautiful nature reserve with a meandering river bordered by cliffs and gum trees, just north of Sydney.

I hand the man behind the counter the booking fee to hire a small boat for the day and he throws me six life jackets. I say to

Xavier, 'It's our special job to start the engine'. His little eyes light up; every firstborn likes 'special jobs'.

He helps me yank on the starter cord of the small engine and it comes to life. The engine's low hum is the only noise you can hear in the valley, with the exception of the birds chirping away.

As we pull away from the pier, I put my arm around my wife, who is sitting next to me at the back of the boat. She is cuddling baby Leon, who is flapping his arms wildly, making a *hee . . . hee . . . hee . . . hee . . .* noise while wearing that delirious grin. Sitting opposite us are Xavier and Luc. They look incredibly handsome in their tiny fluorescent life jackets, like miniature servicemen about to embark on some important mission. In between them is my mum, nursing our picnic basket. Even now, when she gets on a boat she still clings onto the food, but this time she is laughing and joking, making funny faces at the boys.

I look across the water and am mesmerised by the beauty of this magnificent setting. My parents set off on a boat trip many years ago to provide their children and grandchildren a better life. And here we are, thanks to them, enjoying this perfect day.

In that moment I know I am happy. I look up to the blue sky and give thanks.

• In memory of my friend Dave Grant •

In March 2009 my mentor Dave Grant was diagnosed with pancreatic cancer. In January 2010 he passed away at the age of 50. A portion of all profits from the sale of this book will be donated to the Australian Cancer Reasearch Foundation.

When my father was ill I stumbled upon a poem by Rudyard Kipling called *If*. I was ready to dedicate it to my father if he were to 'go somewhere for a long time'. I dedicate it here to Dave. My friend, you are missed.

If

If you can keep your head when all about you
Are losing theirs and blaming it on you,
If you can trust yourself when all men doubt you,
But make allowance for their doubting too;
If you can wait and not be tired by waiting,
Or, being lied about, don't deal in lies,
Or being hated don't give way to hating,
And yet don't look too good, nor talk too wise:

If you can dream—and not make dreams your master;
If you can think—and not make thoughts your aim;
If you can meet with Triumph and Disaster
And treat those two impostors just the same;
If you can bear to hear the truth you've spoken
Twisted by knaves to make a trap for fools,
Or watch the things you gave your life to, broken,
And stoop to build 'em up with worn-out tools:

If you can make one heap of all your winnings
And risk it on one turn of pitch-and-toss,
And lose, and start again at your beginnings
And never breathe a word about your loss;
If you can force your heart and nerve and sinew
To serve your turn long after they are gone,
And so hold on when there is nothing in you
Except the Will which says to them: 'Hold on!'

If you can talk with crowds and keep your virtue,
Or walk with Kings—nor lose the common touch,
If neither foes nor loving friends can hurt you,
If all men count with you, but none too much;
If you can fill the unforgiving minute
With sixty seconds' worth of distance run,
Yours is the Earth and everything that's in it,
And—which is more—you'll be a Man, my son.

Rudyard Kipling

• Acknowledgements •

To the love of my life, Suzanne, who helped me to write many parts of this book. You are, and have always been, my one and only. To our three beautiful boys, Xavier, Luc and Leon—my best buddies in the whole world.

To my mother and father. Thank you both for your love, for your bravery, for being you. To Khoa and Tram, I love you guys, I hope I've told our story well.

For your expertise and brilliance, my publisher Jane Palfreyman, my editors Lauren Finger and Joanne Holliman, my publicist Kelly Fagan and everyone at Allen & Unwin. To my friend Michael Visontay, who taught me how to write a book and helped me with structure and form. To my friend Bruce Griffiths, who helped me with many of the humorous parts of the book. To my friend Marty Wilson, who encouraged me to write a book in the first place and helped me at every stage of the process. And to my mentors: Charles Tarbey, Mike Duff, Christopher Ride, Gerry McShane, Lynne Pearse, Lenny Kovner, Seth Godin, Dave Grant and my agent Lisa Mann. Thank you also to my fantastic manager, Andrew Laing, and everyone at A-List Entertainment.

To all my family and friends who helped at various stages during the writing of this book, especially my uncles Thanh, Huy and Tung, as well as Auntie Trang. Thank you for spending time with me to get the details right, and for being the amazing people that you are.

And finally to my two gorgeous grandmothers—I adore you.